LAKELAND CHURCH WALKS

Peter Donaghy and John Laidler

Published by Sigma Leisure – an imprint of
Sigma Press, 1 South Oak Lane, Wilmslow, Cheshire SK9 6AR, England.

British Library Cataloguing in Publication Data
A CIP record for this book is available from the British Library.

ISBN: 1-85058-761-2

Typesetting and Design by: Sigma Press, Wilmslow, Cheshire.

Cover photograph: St Bartholomew's Church, Loweswater, visited on Walk 7 *(Julian Thurgood)*

Maps: Simon Vandelt

Photographs: the authors

Printed by: MFP Design and Print

Foreword

Simon Jenkins
author of
"England's Thousand Best Churches"

As we enter the third millennium we can find within the walls and graveyards of our churches the history of a people. It is no accident that so many ancient rights of way, now so popular as recreational routes, lead to churches. All these buildings, even those which are no longer at the heart of community life, reflect the love and sacrifices of the countless generations that have striven to maintain them with their labour and their tithes.

These are truly buildings to be treasured, not only as places of worship and architectural interest, but also as rich sources of information about our religious, historical and political culture. Here are galleries of art; here are tales of humble folk and rich patrons alike – a veritable museum of England.

It has always been my wish that like all museums, our parochial churches should be accessible and visitors encouraged. Peter Donaghy and John Laidler have produced an exciting and practical way to combine the exploration of some of England's most beautiful landscapes with the opportunity to visit a variety of churches.

In my own book I included fifteen Cumbrian churches, seven of which are in 'Lakeland' and feature in this guidebook, together with forty-five more. I hope that people will visit these churches and enjoy the walks.

Simon Jenkins

Preface

The abundant attractions of Lakeland ensure that it remains one of the most visited parts of the country. Many visitors, and residents, have an interest in walking and many are part of the growing number of people showing an increasing interest in our cultural heritage – stimulated in part by the transition to the third millennium. Further interest has been generated by the publication of *England's Thousand Best Churches* by Simon Jenkins – many visitors' books contain comments along the lines "Simon Jenkins introduced us to this beautiful church". Our parish churches present a wonderful opportunity to be a starting point from which to explore this heritage. In this book we have combined these interests by describing thirty circular walks based on churches.

Our definition of Lakeland is the area covered by the four Ordinance Survey Outdoor Leisure Maps: The English Lakes, and the walks are grouped under headings corresponding to these maps i.e. North Western area, North Eastern area, South Western area and South Eastern area. All the walks are circular with a variety of landscapes and points of interest, on established rights of way and without foreseeable hazards. Distances range from two miles to thirteen miles. Where possible, particularly for the longer routes, alternative, shorter walks, have been presented to meet the needs of walkers not wishing to complete the full route. However, it has to be recognized that shorter walks might still retain one or more difficult features, for example, a long ascent; an indication of this is given under the heading "terrain" in each section.

We have chosen churches that represent different historical periods and that are of cultural and/or architectural interest and that are spread geographically throughout Lakeland. Some outstanding churches are not included as they are outside the defined area – for example, St Mary and St Bega's at St Bees and St Cuthbert's at Bewcastle. Several walks incorporate visits to more than one church so that, in all, more than 50 churches are described. Most importantly, all the churches used as the focal point of the walks are known to be open for visitors but, in a few exceptional cases, it might be necessary to obtain the key for a church encountered on the route. Car parking is available at or near to all starting points.

The book is divided into 30 sections each covering one walk together with alternative routes where these are presented. For each walk details are given for location, distance, map, terrain and car parking. Under location, the OS reference given is for the church and not for a town or area. Each section also contains a short description of the church or churches, instructions for the walk and an indicative sketch map. The latter uses alphabetical symbols to denote specific points reached on the walk and to provide suitable cross-references to the walk's description.

Descriptions of the churches are not intended to be outlines of the architectural features but instead are subjective accounts of what we felt was merit worthy with reference, where appropriate, to historical events and persons and aspects of architectural and cultural interest. We hope they will serve to whet the walker's appetite to discover more. The instructions for the walks are primarily intended to get the walker round the route and include reference to gates, stiles, bridges and other features and landmarks where these are expected to be helpful to the walker. Although we know that visitors are quite capable of appreciating for themselves the superb views of mountains and lakes they will see, we have not been able to resist making passing mention of these on a number of occasions. Otherwise, in order not to interrupt the sequence of instructions, we have incorporated highlighted vignettes of some of the fascinating people and events associated with the churches and localities visited.

We have tried to ensure that information about the churches and instructions for the walks are correct. However, it is inevitable that changes will occur – for example, signs fall into disrepair, gates and stiles are removed, paths are diverted, trees are felled, new vegetation is grown, restoration work is carried out in churches and some churches are fortunate enough to acquire new furnishings or windows. The visitor needs to make allowance for these changed situations. In addition, adequate time should be allowed for visits to the churches. This might mean making an early start for some of the longer walks!

Finally, a word about respect. Do be careful to respect yourself by ensuring that you are properly clothed, shod and equipped for the conditions you might encounter. It is always advisable to carry the appropriate OS map. Respect the environment in which you are walking by following the country code. For exploration of churches, removal of muddy boots might sometimes be a good idea and visits might have to be deferred if a service is taking place. It may be helpful to have a torch in order to appreciate some of the finer details of the interior of a church. The fact that so many churches remain open for visitors is largely because of the efforts of the local clergy and congregation – which often means just a few people. Their contribution to the maintenance of this part of our heritage deserves our thanks, which we can express by making a suitable donation to their church funds, purchasing the church guidebook and signing the visitors' book.

Peter Donaghy & John Laidler

Acknowledgements

In describing the churches contained in this volume we have had access to a number of important sources which we would like to acknowledge. Anyone attempting to describe English churches cannot ignore Nikolaus Pevsner's *The Buildings of England* series and we are no exceptions. In addition, Simon Jenkins's more recent work, *England's Thousand Best Churches*, has directed us towards some particularly interesting churches within Lakeland while Sir John Betjeman's *Guide to English Parish Churches* has proved to be a further invaluable work of reference.

There are countless books about the Lake District, but four titles have been especially useful to us: Frank Welsh's *Companion Guide to The Lake District* has provided some fascinating and, at times, alternative insights; Bill Mitchell's *Sacred Places of the Lake District* and David Ramshaw's *The English Lakes: Tales from History, Legend and Folklore* have both facilitated an understanding of personalities and customs; and Terry Marsh's *Towns and Villages of Britain: Cumbria* has given us a good general overview.

We are also indebted to the writers of the numerous church guidebooks to which we have had access. These have been listed under the specific church descriptions to which they refer and the authors, where known, have been duly acknowledged. Naturally, we would be happy to include in a future addition any further names brought to our attention.

We are grateful to all those people who helped us when we were walking across Lakeland or visiting the churches – especially all those ministers, churchwardens, stewards and parishioners who so willing responded to our queries. Last but certainly not least, this book would have been impossible without the support and encouragement of our families and, in particular, our wives, Jeanne and Gillian who have walked every mile of the way with us at least once!

Contents

Introduction

The Walks

North West

North East

South West

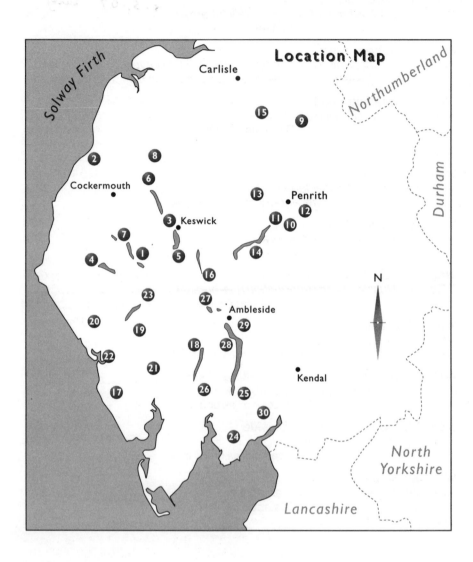

Location Map

Solway Firth

Northumberland

Durham

Carlisle

② 15

9

② 8

Cockermouth ⑥

13 Penrith

③ Keswick

11 12

⑦ ① 10

④ ⑤ 14

16

23 27

20 29

19 Ambleside

22 18 28

21

17 26 25

30

24

N

Kendal

North Yorkshire

Lancashire

Religious and social background

The churches that form the basis of this book reflect some significant aspects of religious and social developments over a period of around 1600 years. However, only a very limited number of these can be referred to in this volume.

As a starting point we need to bear in mind the relative isolation of the geographical area in which the Lakeland churches are located. While the peripheral areas of what is now called Cumbria, bounded by the Solway, the Irish Sea, the Furness peninsula and the north Pennines, have always been receptive to the arrival of new people and cultures, the inner core of the region has been far less accessible. For a long time the rugged nature of the terrain and the existence of dense forests presented natural barriers to communications and the spread of ideas.

However, from the 2nd to the 5th century, the Roman Empire stretched as far as Hadrian's Wall and the Romans provided a network of roads, forts and settlements facilitating the movement of people and the dissemination of ideas. This brought with it the possibility that Christianity too would reach these parts alongside the religious beliefs and deities of the Roman garrisons. By the beginning of the 4th century it seems that Christianity had been firmly established here and although there are no traces of the buildings used for worship, subsequent church builders were certainly happy to take advantage of the well cut masonry that the Romans left behind.

There is some evidence, but also considerable legend, about the impact on the spread of Christianity brought about by the Celtic saints. Uncertainty remains as to whether their presence was real or merely the useful figment of subsequent imagination, but church dedications and related place names suggest that they had a significant influence. According to tradition, St Ninian founded a monastery at Whithorn in nearby Galloway in AD398. He studied under St Martin at Tours, which may explain the dedication of Martindale's old church (Walk 14), and he himself possibly visited Ninekirks near Brougham (Walk 12). St Patrick is said to have been in Patterdale in the 5th century.

The 7th century is clearly identified with missionary activities from Ireland, Scotland and Northumbria and it was during this period that Christianity gained a firm foothold. St Kentigern is thought to have preached at Crosthwaite near Keswick (Walk 3); St Bega is linked with St Bees and with Bassenthwaite (Walk 3); St Cuthbert was granted land at Cartmel (Walk 24).

There is strong evidence of the cross-fertilisation of Christianity with Norse influence in the shape of Celtic crosses with their intricate patterns which show how Viking symbolism was incorporated into the missionary message, as for example at Gosforth (Walk 20). Likewise there are baptismal fonts with similar symbolic motifs, for instance in Bridekirk (Walk 6).

However, it was not until the second millennium, and the coming of the Normans in 1066, that many of the church buildings and much of today's parochial organisation came into being. In the wake of the Norman invasion the barons established territorial divisions and political stability within which the Church could operate. It is probable that Norman stone churches were frequently constructed on the site of earlier churches built of less durable materials, as was the case, for example at Waberthwaite (Walk 22).

The monasteries provided a focal point and an impetus for the spread of Christianity. In addition, some religious orders, such as the Augustinians and the Cistercians made important contributions to economic development. The extensive land holdings, for example, of Cartmel Priory (Walk 24) and Furness Abbey resulted in the establishment of dependent chapels and farm granges sometimes many miles away such as Colton (Walk 26). The monks of St Bees established chapels at Ennerdale (Walk 4), Loweswater (Walk 7), Eskdale (Walk 19) and Wasdale (Walk 23) in the 12th century.

While a network of footpaths reveals many of the traditional routes which people followed to church, there were circumstances in which distance became an impediment to worship, and so permission was granted to establish churches in closer proximity to populations. This gave rise to the creation of "chapels-of-ease", such as St Anthony's at Cartmel Fell (Walk 25). However, the "mother church" usually reserved the right to conduct funerals and the so-called "coffin roads" indicate the journeys that sometimes had to be undertaken in order to bury the dead.

It is generally felt that Henry VIII's final break with Rome in 1534, followed by the Dissolution of the Monasteries shortly thereafter, initially had less impact here than elsewhere. In time, wealthy families, such as the Cliffords (Walk 12), the Le Flemings (Walk 18), the Dacres (Walk 11), the Howards (Walk 13) and the Lowthers (Walk 10) replaced the religious orders as patrons of the relatively small numbers of churches in the region. At the same time changes in ecclesiastical practices were not necessarily pursued with great vigour.

The 16th and 17th centuries were characterised by Acts of Parliament, which sought to bring about uniformity of religious observances, conformity with the established church and loyalty to the monarchy. Not everyone, however, was prepared to accept this level of restriction. The latter part of the 17th century saw dissenters or non-conformists coming together in different guises and the arrival of alternative forms of worship and different styles of buildings.

Soldiers in Cromwell's New Model Army are believed to have introduced the Baptist movement to the north-west. This later came to manifest itself at Tottlebank where a small number first gathered as the "Church of Christ" in 1669 (Walk 26). George Fox and his Society of Friends or Quakers attracted many adherents, initially meeting in private houses and then more openly in "Meeting Houses", at places such as Colthouse near Hawkshead (Walk 28). Then there were political considerations stemming, for example, from the Jacobite risings of 1715 and 1745 which suggested a revival of Roman Catholicism, practised only clandestinely at that time. It is therefore perhaps not surprising to find the royal coat of arms in churches in order to leave parishioners in no doubt as to where their loyalty lay, as, for example, in St Bega's at Bassenthwaite Lake (Walk 3).

The second half of the 18th century brought further non-conformist growth through John Wesley, a frequent visitor to the area. The impact of his missionary zeal was particularly felt after his death in 1791 when the industrial revolution was in full swing and great social and economic changes were underway. The new urban working class, owing no allegiance to the established hierarchy, was particularly attracted by Methodism which seemed to be more appropriate for their needs and more flexible in building places of worship near centres of population.

Tourism was beginning to have an influence towards the end of the 18th century. William Wordsworth's "Guide to the Lakes" was first published in 1810 and by 1835 there had been five editions. Undoubtedly the poet was influential in making the area more "fashionable" and people from all over the world still flock to visit his grave in Grasmere churchyard ((Walk 27). Other leading literary and intellectual figures, such as Robert Southey (Walk 3) and John Ruskin (Walk 18) also did much in the 19th century to make people aware of the attractiveness of this corner of England. The advent of the railways and development of road networks made the area more accessible and new churches were built in response, as was the case with St Mary's at Ambleside (Walk 29). Meanwhile, campaigners such as Canon Rawnsley (Walks 3 and 28) strove to defend the environment from excessive intrusion.

The Victorian period was also characterised by attempts to rebuild and restore many church buildings in order to cope with demographic changes, or simply at the whim of individuals. Churches were rebuilt, for example, at Ainstable (Walk 9), Newlands (Walk 5) and Wasdale Head (Walk 23). At the same time many existing churches were subject to considerable restoration and modification, sometimes to the detriment of their original artistic wealth. New churches were also built at the behest of individuals, for example, in Wreay (Walk 15) and Low Wray (Walk 28).

The 20th century undoubtedly saw a general fall off in church attendance. With this came the problem of maintaining or closing church buildings. Closure of many Methodist chapels followed the merger of branches of Methodism in 1932, and similarly the fusion of the Congregationalists and the Presbyterians in 1972 into the United Reformed Church, led to a reduction in church owned property. It is therefore not uncommon to come across many desirable modern dwellings that ironically have been the result of "conversion".

The historical heritage of the Church of England has been maintained with a struggle. Shortage of clergy has led to alternative forms of organisation such as team ministries or parishes sharing the same incumbent and some churches have been declared redundant, for example at Ireby (Walk 8). However, the efforts of local congregations have enabled the vast majority of churches to remain open as places of worship at the beginning of the third millennium.

Church Architecture

Basic church structure

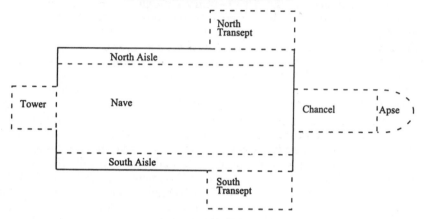

Architectural terms

Apse: a semi-circular addition to the chancel at the east end of a church.

Arcade: a number of arches sustained by columns usually dividing the nave from the aisles..

Bellcote: a turret on the roof where bells are hung.

Capital: the top of a column, usually carved.

Chancel: the eastern end of the church where the main altar is situated. It is often divided from the nave by an arch (chancel arch).

Gothic: a style of architecture found approximately between the 12th and 16th centuries, its most significant feature being pointed arches. This style became increasingly popular again in the Victorian period.

Hatchment: a diamond-shaped tablet showing the coat of arms of a deceased person.

Lancet window: a narrow window with a pointed top.

Light: the individual compartment of a window.

Misericord: a shelf under hinged choir seat to support a person when standing,

Nave: the body or main part of the church.

Norman: a style of architecture introduced into England following the Norman Conquest of 1066, its most significant feature being rounded arches.

Piscina: basin in or on a wall in which church vessels are washed.

Reredos: a decorated panel behind an altar.

Sanctuary: the part of the chancel containing the altar.

Screen: a wooden or stone structure wholly or partially dividing the chancel from the nave.

Single chamber church: a church with no significant division between the nave and the chancel.

Transepts: extensions on the north and south of the church which give a church a cross (cruciform) shape.

Transom: a horizontal divider between two sections of a window.

11 · 5 · 06

Walk 1: Buttermere

Scribe, sheep and secrets

Location: St James's Church (NY176170) is on the outskirts of the village of Buttermere at the junction of the B5289 and the Newlands Pass road.

Distance: 4 miles.

Map: OS Outdoor Leisure 4: The English Lakes North Western area.

Terrain: Mainly on paths and grassy tracks with two long gradual ascents.

Church: St James, Buttermere.

Car parking: There is a small car parking area near the church. Alternative parking is available in the Lake District National Park car park in the lane to the right of the Fish Hotel and there is a National Trust Car Park on the northern edge of the village on the B5289.

The Church

This is a very small church, with a bellcote and a tiny chancel standing on a little rocky mound at the junction of the roads leading to the Honister and Newlands passes. It is in a superb position, surrounded by magnificent Lakeland fells between the lakes of Buttermere and Crummock Water.

The present building was completed in 1841 and restored in 1930 but an earlier church on the site dates back to 1507. Standing nearby is the former school now used as a church room. This was built in 1871 as a replacement for an older schoolroom and was in use as the school until 1950.

The little church of St James, Buttermere

The population of the parish, like the church, is very small, and, like others of similar size, was staffed in earlier centuries by a non-ordained assistant called a reader who received 20 shillings a year, basic clothing and other rights such as goosegate, the right to run his geese on the common. A curate who served here until 1736, who would have received similar rights, but who was an ordained priest was the redoubtable "Wonderful Walker" (see Walk 21, Seathwaite Church).

Entrance to the porch is by means of a wrought iron gate depicting a shepherd and lambs. The Christian symbolism seems particularly appropriate to the church's surroundings. Inside, there is a single chamber with plain walls and fine oak pews, carved communion rail, pulpit and roof beams. There are a number of memorial tablets and inscriptions on the walls and furnishings but, overall, there remains an impression of peaceful simplicity.

Among the other features of interest are:

❖ The small stone font with a wooden cover from 1930 given by the children of the parish who were at school in that year.

❖ On a window sill, immediately on the right when entering, a plaque in memory of Alfred Wainwright, the famous author of Lake District fell walking guides, with a view of Haystacks where his ashes were scattered (see below).

❖ The 1914-1918 War Memorial and wooden cross on the north wall listing seven men from this small community.

❖ At the east end, the stained glass window depicting Mary and Martha dedicated to Elizabeth Attlee, wife of a former vicar. She became a missionary and died in Bethlehem in1892.

Information available in the church:

❶ Hand-held information board.

> *Alfred Wainright chose Haystacks as the fell where his ashes would be scattered. The plaque in the church reminds us that he was a "fellwalker, guide book author and illustrator who loved this valley". His books have won thousands of converts to Lakeland's attractions. Not that the great man would have been bothered about speaking to any of them! As Bill Mitchell points out "Wainwright was a loner in his fell-top world, lost in his own thoughts, not suffering fools gladly, speaking – Quaker style – only when the spirit moved him". However, he did have an impish sense of humour. His biographer, Hunter Davies, reminds us of, perhaps, the best illustration of this quoting Wainwright's own words about his proposed final resting place: "... And if you, dear reader, should get a bit of grit in your boot as you are crossing Hay Stacks in the years to come, please treat it with respect. It might be me".*

The Walk

From the bottom of the church steps **(A)** turn right and follow the road as it bears right to come to a junction. Turn left and walk to the Fish Hotel. 200 years ago, this was the home of Mary Robinson, the Beauty of Buttermere.

Mary Robinson was the Fish Hotel's landlord's daughter who served at table for her father. She was a stunning young woman who became known as the Beauty of Buttermere. Her fame spread after a visitor made mention of her in his published travel journal. In 1802, she married Lieutenant-Colonel the Honourable Alexander Augustus Hope. Unfortunately, the groom had been keeping secrets from her. He was not the colonel but an impostor named John Hatfield and had a wife still living and several children from two marriages. He was later hanged in Carlisle, not for bigamy but forgery – a harsh penalty even by standards of the early nineteenth century. Mary remarried in 1808, lived as a farmer's wife, and had four children. She died in 1837 at Caldbeck where she is buried. Her story has been told in several novels, most recently by Melvyn Bragg in "The Maid of Buttermere".

Go into the lane to the right of the hotel and walk through the car parking area to come to a metal gate. Go through the gate (the reference "no footpath" does not refer to the route you are following) and immediately turn right through another gate. There is a footbridge in front of you with a sign for Sykes Farm. Do not go over the bridge but turn left and proceed along the path with the wire fence on your left and the beck on your right. Continue on the path, passing through another gate, as it bears right to run alongside the beck with Crummock Water appearing ahead to arrive at a stile with a National Trust notice. Cross the stile and footbridge and turn right in the direction indicated to "Buttermere Village via Longhow Wood". Proceed along the gravelly path with the beck on your right and after a couple of hundred metres follow the path as it bears left to ascend between the trees and through a kissing gate. Carry on as the path levels out and exit via a kissing gate onto the B5289 **(B)**.

Turn left and walk 100 metres or so to take a stony path off to the right. The path goes uphill and then descends to rejoin the road, near Woodhouse on the opposite side, having nicely cut off the corner. Bear right and walk along the road for 200 metres with Crummock Water in view on the left. Look out for the public bridleway sign on the right to "Buttermere Hause". Take the bridleway as it climbs steadily, offering spectacular views of the southern end of Crummock Water. Keep to the path, ignoring tracks going off to the right, until it reaches its highest point, when the northern half of Crummock Water comes into view. Follow the path as it descends quite steeply to arrive at the road. Turn right and walk the short distance to the small car parking area on your right. There is a National Trust sign showing that you are at Rannerdale **(C)**. A battle which took place here was described in a book by Nicholas Size.

Nicholas Size was a notable "incomer" who lived in Buttermere and took a great interest in local affairs. In 1930, he suggested that the old pews removed during the restoration of the church in that year be placed along the roads and footpaths of the area. His idea was vehemently opposed from within and outside the parish. A much more successful venture by him was the publication in the same year of "The Secret Valley". In the book, which is based on fact but with fictional embellishment, the secret valley is the Buttermere Valley itself, stretching along Crummock Water to its head at Gatesgarth. The book describes the defence by the English/Norse inhabitants on their chosen ground against Saxon and later Norman incursions. A notable success being the Battle of Rannerdale in the 11th century, when the Normans were led into a bloody ambush in the narrow Rannerdale Valley.

Walk past the National Trust sign and follow the path with a stone wall on your left and the heights of Rannerdale Knotts on your right. The path comes to a kissing gate near to which is a notice board with a map of the area. Go through the kissing gate following the path, again with the stone wall on your left and Rannerdale Knotts on your right. The path bears to the right

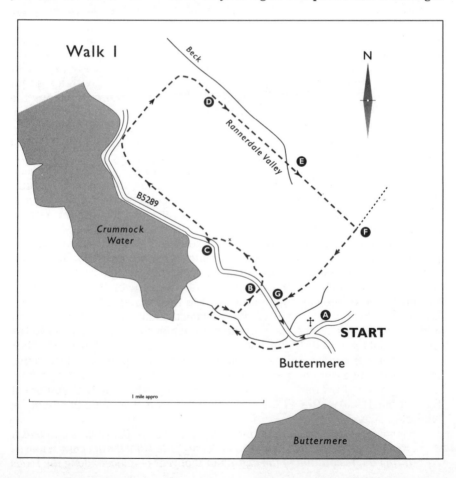

and the remains of a broken stone wall appear on the left. Eventually, you meet a stream coming in from the left. Carry on in the direction you have been walking, alongside the fast flowing stream on your left, until you reach a footbridge **(D)**.

Do not go over the footbridge but continue on the path as it goes through a wooden gate in a wall on the right. Turn left and walk along the well-defined path as it enters the valley between High Rannerdale on the left and the ridge of Rannerdale Knotts on the right. Keep on the clear path for about 800 metres, ignoring a footbridge with a stile nearby, until the path bears to the left to drop down to cross a narrow beck **(E)**. Continue on the path, which is clearly visible ahead, as it veers to the left with the beck a little further away on the right. The path now begins a gradual climb and it might be appropriate to take a breath stop (or two!) and look back as more of Crummock Water comes into view and, eventually, beyond Crummock Water, Loweswater can be seen in the distance. It is easy to imagine this hidden valley as the place where the Normans were ambushed. In bluebell time there is a mass of colour here and many people refer to this (rather than the Buttermere Valley) as the secret valley. As the path emerges from the valley, another track crosses the path you are on. At this point, you need to turn right **(F)**.

The northern end of Buttermere is now in view in front of you with the water of Sourmilk Gill flowing down the side of Dodd into the lake. You need to walk in the direction of the waterfall. There are a number of alternative descents but you can keep to the left-hand path as it goes down towards the white houses of Buttermere village. The impressive heights of Haystacks lie at the southern end of Buttermere. The path underfoot is grassy until it comes to a stone wall on your left. Follow the path, keeping the wall and then a wire fence on your left. Go through the wooden gate, just before the first cottage, and continue on the path as it skirts behind the houses to emerge onto a road **(G)**.

If you have parked at the National Trust car park, this is up to the right, on the left-hand side of the road. Otherwise, turn left and walk back through the village to the church and the end of the walk.

Walk 2: Crosscanonby

Seascape, swingers and smugglers

Location: St John the Evangelist's Church (NY069390) is at Crosscanonby, about 3 miles north-east of Maryport, on a minor road from Crosby off the A596.

Distance: Walk 2(a), Crosscanonby, Blue Dial Farm and Maryport Golf Club: 4¾ miles; Walk 2(b), Crosscanonby and Maryport Golf Club: 3 miles.

Map: OS Outdoor Leisure 4: The English Lakes North Western area.

Terrain: Both walks are mainly on the level on a coastal path and over a golf course. Walk 2(b) involves about a mile on a minor road but avoids the stiles of Walk 2(a).

Church: St John the Evangelist, Crosscanonby.

Car parking: There is parking beside the church.

The Church

This delightful little church, stands on a rise at the entrance to the small hamlet of Crosscanonby and from the churchyard there are views over the Solway Firth. Not far away are the remains of a Roman fort, evidence that this was once a far outpost of the Roman Empire.

There is considerable speculation about the origins of the site. Stones found in the building and in the grounds point to the previous existence of a Roman structure; a Viking hog back gravestone lies outside the south-east corner of the church, and remnants of ancient crosses and other stones are

St John the Evangelist, Crosscanonby

exhibited in the porch. There are even suggestions that St Ninian and St Kentigern may have been early visitors here.

However, the present church dates from about 1130 and although it has been restored and refurbished many times, it is still largely Norman in style with substantial Victorian overtones. Direct evidence of the Norman influence can be found in the shape of the window frame in the south wall of the chancel and the small crude arch located in the wall above the arcade which leads to the south aisle and chapel. The aisle itself was added in the 13th century.

The chancel arch is a splendid piece of Roman work which, apparently, once marked the entrance to the quarters of the commander of the garrison at nearby Maryport. The niches on either side of it are believed to have held Roman statues. It was incorporated into the present church in the 18th century by Humphrey Stenhouse of Maryport.

The church clearly owes a lot to the patronage of the Stenhouse family and they are well remembered in a number of wall tablets on the north wall of the chancel. Their family pew was used in the 1930s to reconstruct the minstrels' gallery and the carved oak dating from 200 years earlier makes a fine show.

Among the other features of interest are:

❖ The 13th-century carved alabaster font at the rear of the church.

❖ The framed texts on either side of the walls of the nave.

❖ The coat of arms of George II on the north wall, a reminder of where parishioners' loyalty should lie.

❖ The quilted banner on the south wall made by parishioners in 1993.

❖ The war memorial beyond the east wall, a poignant reminder of the impact of war on small communities.

Information available in the church:

❶ Board with historical notes and data on the west wall.

❶ *The history of St John the Evangelist Crosscanonby.*

The Walks
Walk 2(a), Crosscanonby, Blue Dial Farm and Maryport Golf Club: 4¾ miles

After visiting St John's Church **(A)** exit through the lych-gate, turn left and then bear right to pass in front of the cottages along the higher of the two roads. At the end of the roadway, bear left down the gravel track to a fingerpost "Blue Dial". Follow in the direction of the sign and as the track bears right, cross the waymarked stile next to the metal gate **(B)**.

Proceed diagonally right up the field and through a waymarked gateway. Go straight across the next field to take a double stile next to a metal gate. Now take a moment to admire the sea view ahead to the left and to identify the barns of Blue Dial Farm just inland. You now need to take several stiles in

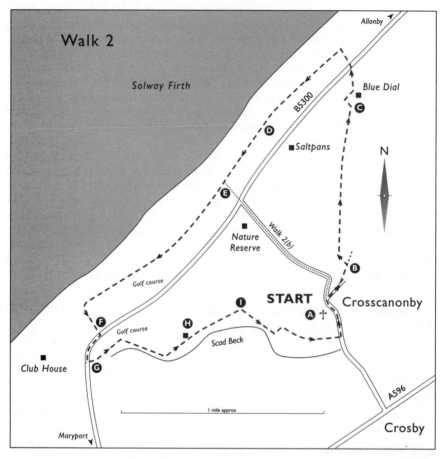

order to cross a series of fields descending in the direction of these buildings. Your way should be clear but here is some help just in case!

Cross the next field and take the stile about a third of the way along the boundary hedgerow. Walk down to the bottom of the next field and cross the double stile partially hidden, again about a third of the way along the hedgerow. Now cross the next field diagonally right in the direction of Blue Dial Farm to take a waymarked stile next to a metal gate. Proceed diagonally left across the next field to a footbridge in the opposite corner. There are stiles to cross at either end of the footbridge and a waymark sign as you exit. Once more, proceed diagonally left across the next field to a waymark sign next to a metal gate in the opposite corner at Blue Dial Farm. Go through the gate and bear right to pass to the left of the barn. This section can be very muddy and there may be temporary wire fencing. However, you need to make for the fingerpost in the corner down to the left where you cross a stile onto the Maryport-Allonby road (C).

Cross the road with care to pick up a track a few metres to the right to make your way across the grassland towards the coastline. Turn left on the coastal path and follow the clear path keeping the sea on your right and the Maryport-Allonby road on your left. At a Cumbria Coastal Way sign, you might like to make a detour to visit two interesting historical sites and to get a better view of the horizon. You need to cross the busy road with care as you are very near a corner **(D)**.

Here you will find a noticeboard which provides an interesting explanation of the local saltpans. The saltpans were important from medieval times until the early part of the 18th century. They were owned by the Stenhouse family of Maryport, patrons of Crosscanonby Church and there is reference to a Salt Officer who died in 1730 and who is buried in the churchyard.

A short climb up the steps takes you to an observation platform where you can read about the Roman fort which once stood there and see the outline of the excavations.

Looking across the sea you should be able to make out the Galloway Hills. The coastline then stretches west towards Whithorn where, according to legend, St Ninian established the first centre of Celtic Christianity in AD398.

After this brief interlude, continue along the coastal path until you come level with a road junction on your left and a minor road leads back to Crosscanonby **(E)**.

Here you will find the small nature reserve of Crosscanonby Carr (with picnic tables and a toilet block), a few metres up on the right-hand side of the minor road. It is worth a short detour to explore it and to read the explanatory information boards about the plant and wildlife on this reclaimed site.

To continue on the walk, proceed along the coastal path until you eventually arrive at Maryport Golf Course. The path runs along the right-hand side of the course and you need to beware of flying golf balls! It is also advisable to respect the etiquette of the game and keep still and quiet if golfers are playing shots nearby. After a few hundred metres carefully bear left across the golf course on a clear raised track and exit through a gate onto the main road **(F)**.

Bear right and follow the road on the grass verge by the side of the golf course for about a hundred and fifty metres. Cross the road with care just before the cemetery and take the public bridleway signposted "Crosscanonby" **(G)**.

Now you need to walk around the perimeter of the course again with the same caution as before. Keep close to the old hedgerow on your right until you come to some appropriate warning signs: "Golfers be aware of public footpath" and "Walkers beware of golf course". At this point, go through a gap in the wire fence and up the ramp leading to the sixth tee. Continue along the side of the course with the Scad Beck on your right and keep to the perimeter of the course following the red marker posts until you reach a green shed **(H)**.

(The public footpath, which pre-dates the extension of the golf course to this side of the main road, technically passes further to the left and goes across various fairways but custom, practice and prudence indicates that this is now the most appropriate route to follow).

Go to the right of the shed, pass between two old gateposts and within a hundred metres or so go through a gate with public bridleway and "smugglers' route" waymarks. (The smugglers' route is a relatively new 27-mile walk from Maryport to Ireby). Ahead, in the distance, you should be able to see the farm buildings of Crosscanonby and possibly the bellcote of the church. Continue straight ahead and then, after going through a waymarked gateway, turn right **(I)**.

Proceed along the track with the beck again on your right and at the end of the field, follow the waymark direction by bearing left with a hedge still on you right. Pass through another waymarked gate and bear right to walk passing the sewage plant on you left. Keep on the clear track and, as you get closer to the farm, you will see the church behind. Go through the gate, then turn right to go through a double metal gate and then walk up the track for a hundred metres or so to exit onto the road. Turn left and follow the road a short distance to St John's Church and the end of the walk.

Walk 2(b), Crosscanonby and Maryport Golf Club: 3 miles

After visiting St John's Church **(A)** exit through the lych-gate, turn left and follow the minor road for about a mile down to the coast. Just before you meet the B5300 Maryport-Allonby road at T-junction, you pass Crosscanonby Carr Nature Reserve (see above). At the T-junction, cross over the road with care to join the coastal path and turn left to follow Walk 2(a) from **(E)** above. This takes you along the coast, over the golf course and back to St John's Church. However, before doing this you might like to make a short detour to visit the site of the salt pans and the Roman fort as described above. To do this, turn right, rather than left, follow the coastal path for about 800 metres, visit the sites, then retrace your steps back to **(E)**.

Walk 3: Crosthwaite (Keswick) and St Bega's (Bassenthwaite Lake)

Savers of souls, sawmill and sword

Location: St Kentigern's Church, Crosthwaite, (NY258243) is just off the B5289 at the north-west end of Keswick.

Distance: Walk 3(a), Crosthwaite and St Bega's: 10 miles; Walk 3(b), Crosthwaite only: 5 miles; Walk 3(c), St Bega's only: 6 miles.

Map: OS Outdoor Leisure 4: The English Lakes North Western area.

Terrain: These walks are principally on public footpaths through farmland and on tracks through Forest Enterprise land. There are some steep uphill sections on Walks 3(a) and 3(c).

Churches: St Kentigern, Crosthwaite; St Bega, Bassenthwaite Lake.

Car parking: For Walks 3(a) and 3(b) park at St Kentigern's Church, Crosthwaite (Keswick). For Walk 3(c) park on the minor road to Applethwaite off the A591 near Chestnut Cottage between Millbeck and the A591.

The Churches

St Kentigern, Crosthwaite

The church of St Kentigern stands at Crosthwaite at the north-west entrance to Keswick, away from the hustle and bustle of the centre and the tourists, from where there are splendid views over to Skiddaw, Whinlatter and Newlands. This is believed to have been the site where the missionary bishop Kentigern (or Mungo) planted his cross in a clearing (thwaite) in the middle of the sixth century.

A succession of buildings has been developed here with some stones of the early 12th century providing the oldest traces. A helpful plan in the church porch graphically illustrates the modifications, which have taken place over the centuries. However, the basic form of the present church was established in 1523.

Today the church is a substantial structure, solid and rectangular on the outside, but warm and welcoming on the inside. Despite its deep sense of medieval history, it is to the Victorians that the church owes most of its present day appearance. A major restoration and embellishment programme carried out in the mid-19th century has left it with many fine stained glass windows and elaborate wall tablets which tell lots of stories.

Two particularly significant figures associated with St Kentigern's are Canon Rawnsley, a co-founder of the National Trust and Robert Southey, the 19th-century Poet Laureate. Canon Rawnsley was vicar from 1883 to 1917 and there is a dedication around the wooden panelling of the bapistry to commemorate his silver jubilee in the parish, as well as a wall tablet in his memory nearby (see also Walk 28, St Margaret, Low Wray).

Robert Southey (1714-1843) was a devout parishioner here for some forty years until his death in 1843. There is a memorial effigy of him in white marble in the south aisle with an epitaph by his friend William Wordsworth.

St Kentigern, Crosthwaite

His gravestone, restored with help from the Brazilian Government (there is an explanation of this in the porch), stands in the churchyard by the south-west corner of the church.

This church is obviously well looked after and offers an extensive collection of guidebooks and leaflets on its numerous attractions. Here in St Kentigern there is clearly a great deal to see.

Among the other features of interest are:

❖ The 14th-century font displayed on a marble plinth in the south-west corner.

❖ The nine stone crosses within circles on the inside walls and the twelve such crosses on the outside walls that commemorate the consecration of the church, a collection which is unique in England. There are good examples of the interior crosses near the windows on the north wall.

❖ The kneelers with their spiritual and biblical symbols in the Ormathwaite pew in the north-east chapel.

❖ The stained glass east window by the famous designer Kempe (see Walk 8, All Saints, Bolton). St Kentigern is portrayed in the south light and St Herbert of Derwentwater is in the north light.

❖ The mosaic floor of the sanctuary reflecting the story of St Kentigern with emblems that are also echoed elsewhere in the church and on the main gate.

Information available in the church:

A useful selection of literature including:

❶ *History of Crosthwaite Parish Church,* Tom Wilson, revised by J.W. Kaye.

St Bega, Bassenthwaite Lake

ℹ *The most active volcano in Europe: A short life of Canon Hardwicke Drummond Rawnsley.*

St Bega, Bassenthwaite Lake

This is a small, simple chapel in an idyllic setting, a few metres from Bassenthwaite Lake. If you are fortunate enough to arrive when there are no other visitors you will find here a true haven of peace and tranquillity. The silence is only broken by the rushing water of the stream flowing down to the lake and the cry of birds.

Over the years, the church received many distinguished visitors. The poet Tennyson came in the early 19th century, and it is believed that it was here on the shore of Bassenthwaite Lake that he wrote about King Arthur's sword, Excalibur. Visitors are now welcomed by a sign in five languages. This is certainly a place to pause and ponder. Several entries in the visitors' book refer to St Bega's as an "oasis of peace".

A plain cross stands outside the entrance to the ancient churchyard and it is believed that a church has been here since AD950. It is thought that it marks the spot where St Bega, the daughter of a 7th-century Irish chieftain resided or was buried. The story of Bega is told in the leaflet available in the church, in a booklet available at The Old Sawmill Tearoom and in Melvyn Bragg's book *Credo*.

The neat and intimate interior of the church provides a contrast to the more ornate St Kentigern's at Crosthwaite. There is less to see but possibly more to savour. It is mainly Norman in style with some 14th and 16th century characteristics. However, it owes a lot to the major and sensitive restoration that took place in 1874, at the instigation of Henry Spedding. The dedications on the stained glass windows give some indication of the connections

of the church with the Speddings of nearby Mirehouse, as too does the graveyard.

Among the other features of interest are:

❖ The 14th-century baptismal font.

❖ The prayer-story of St Bega on the north window sill.

❖ The medieval lead crucifix on the north side of the chancel arch.

❖ The Norman chancel arch.

❖ The wrought iron holder for an hour glass to time the length of sermons,
on the south pillar of the chancel arch.

❖ The coat of arms of George II over the archway to the south aisle to remind
people of their loyalty to the English crown at the time of the 1745 rebellion.

Further information available in the church:

❶ A leaflet, *The Parish Church of St Bega, Bassenthwaite.*

The Walks
Walk 3(a), Crosthwaite and St Bega:10 miles

After leaving St Kentigern's churchyard through the main gate **(A)** turn left
and continue straight ahead to follow the public footpath "Mill Beck" as it
gently ascends and passes the school on your right. Go through the kissing
gate and walk down the field slightly to the right to go under an old railway
bridge. Then cross a ladder stile and proceed with care to cross the A66 road
to the public footpath sign "Thrushwood ¼ mile". Go over the footbridge and
over a ladder stile. Cross the field to take a stile in the fence and then climb
the path between the houses to emerge onto the road in Thrushwood at
Charnwood Lodge **(B)**.

Cross the road and, following the public footpath sign, go through a kissing gate to follow the path a short way between the trees. Pass through
another kissing gate and then go over the duck boarding into a field with a
fence on your left. Pass through a metal gateway in the fence ahead and bear
left round the farm shed to pass through a kissing gate. Continue straight
ahead with the fence and an old hedgerow on your left and follow the line of
the fence as it turns left. After a short distance pass through a gate, then over
a footbridge and follow the path for a few hundred metres, with trees on your
right and a fence on your left, to pass through another gate. Bear left, cross
the stream by the old stone footbridge and proceed a few metres to meet the
road at Applethwaite **(C)**.

Turn right and then immediately left at the telephone box. Continue
down the road between the houses for about three hundred and fifty metres
and immediately after Orchard House leave the road and go over the parking
area in front of Derwent Lea. There is a public footpath sign here but it is half
hidden by ivy. Cross the stile into a field and continue straight ahead with
the fence on your left. Pass through the gate in the wall and over the next

field with a plantation on your left making for the farm buildings ahead. Pass through the kissing gate and follow the marker posts that lead around the right-hand side of the buildings. Go over the footbridge and through a kissing gate just beyond the sign for Millbeck. Cross the field with the hedge on your left to a further kissing gate. Now proceed ahead with a hedge on your right towards the farm. Cross the stile next to the gate at the left of the farm buildings and make your way between the buildings. It can be quite muddy here. Follow the farm track through a gate marked "footpath" and onto the road. Turn right up the road to a T-junction at Millbeck village hall with the chateau-like building beyond. Turn left over the bridge and continue along the road until you reach a lay-by on the right about a hundred metres beyond Chestnut Cottage **(D)**.

At the end of the lay-by, leave the road by some steps on the right. Follow the public footpath sign to cross a footbridge over a stream and then a stile over a fence. Follow the path as it makes its way through the bracken. After a short distance, the path bears right towards the right-hand corner of the wood ahead as you continue on the clear path with the trees on the left. The path soon begins to climb steeply through the bracken towards the forest ahead and away from the wood and the road below. After a while it brings you to a fence with a wall behind and trees beyond. Continue upwards and, where the fence and the wall more or less converge, go over the stile and through the wall to enter Thornthwaite Forest **(E)**.

Now turn left, cross the stream and at a junction a few metres ahead take the path, which bears right and upwards, between the trees, ignoring the track down to the left. Continue winding your way gradually upwards until you eventually reach a clearing as the track broadens out. Ignore a track off to the right and continue on the main track as it bears left across the clearing and then soon passes over the beck. The track becomes a more obvious forest road as it contours round the slate lined hillside and eventually reaches a clearing where another forest road descends from the right to join it. Here there are good views of both Derwentwater and Bassenthwaite Lake. Continue straight ahead on the main forest road as it gradually descends. After about a mile, as the road completes a horseshoe bend to the left, leave the forest road and follow the path off to the right marked "Café & Car Park" **(F)**.

Follow this path through the trees and past a further sign for the café and the car park to reach a T-junction. Turn left and follow the Skill Beck down to the picnic tables, the toilets and The Old Sawmill Tearoom (which houses an interesting display of information about the original sawmill) **(G)**.

To continue, cross the road with caution and take the public footpath through a gate at the left of the entrance lodge to Mirehouse.

Mirehouse was originally built in the 17th century. It was frequently visited by many of the great literary figures of the 19th century, such as Wordsworth, Southey and Tennyson, after the Spedding family moved there from nearby Armathwaite Hall. The Speddings still live at Mirehouse and the house, which contains a fascinating collection of original furniture and manu-

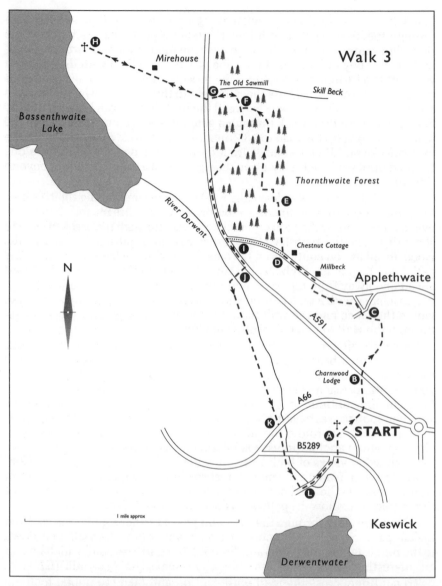

scripts, is open to the public on certain days. The Speddings were succeeded at Armathwaite Hall by the Vane family. Both of these families have memorials in St Bega's Church.

Proceed down the driveway, bearing left at the end round the buildings, and shortly St Bega's Church comes into view by the lakeside. Take the left fork to reach a gate and follow the sign across a field to the church **(H)**.

After visiting the church, make your way back via the footpath past Mirehouse to The Old Sawmill Tearoom **(G)**. Once at The Old Sawmill, you need to retrace your steps back to the forest road **(F)**. To do this, climb back up the path to the right of the Skill Beck for about 300 metres and take the first path on the right. Follow this to a junction of paths where the forest trail bears left and continue straight ahead on the minor path to rejoin the forest road, at the point at which you left on your downward journey **(F)**.

Now turn right and continue along the main forest road as it descends and winds down to the Keswick-Carlisle road. After the barrier at the end of the forest road, take a path off to the left, just before the main road. Follow this path as it makes its way parallel to the road and eventually reaches some wooden steps which descend to the road. Turn left and follow the roadside path past White Stones to where a minor road to Millbeck, Applethwaite, Skiddaw joins from the left **(I)**.

Now cross over the Keswick-Carlisle road with caution and proceed by the side of the road a few hundred metres, passing Dancing Gate on the opposite side, to take the first opening on your right by the public footpath sign "Portinscale; Braithwaite" **(J)**.

Go over the stile by the gate and follow the farm track to cross the River Derwent over a metal bridge. At the end of the metal bridge, turn immediately left through the waymarked gate. Follow the path, with the river on your left, via a number of stiles/gates until you reach a notice "No right of way along this river bank". At this point, go diagonally right across the field. At the end of an old hedgerow pass an old gate post and follow the waymark sign across a field to a signpost. Now pass through the gate and bear left at the sign "Portinscale". Continue along the track to a waymarked kissing gate by a gate and follow the farm track to cross a stile by a gate and just before the farm buildings take the waymarked path through a gate on the left signposted "Portinscale ½ mile". Go over the field to cross a stile in the fence opposite. Bear right to the riverbank, passing the "private land" sign on your left, and follow the riverbank a short way to cross two stiles in quick succession. Now proceed straight ahead keeping the river close by on the left to cross a stile at a dismantled railway bridge. Go round the base of the old bridge, climb the steps and go through the gate. Continue along the riverbank and go under the A66 road bridge **(K)**.

Now proceed ahead to cross a stile at the next road bridge and climb a short way to a further stile which takes you to the B5289. Cross the road and take the stile opposite. Descend the path and cross another stile to return to the riverbank. Portinscale lies ahead to the right. Proceed ahead with the river on your left crossing two further stiles to leave the field by a gate. Turn left and cross the river by the suspension bridge **(L)**.

Continue straight ahead on the paved path alongside the metalled road, ignoring the path off to the right to Keswick as the path becomes separated from the road by a grass verge. Go over the footbridge and keep on the path as it bears right beside the B5289 towards Keswick. After a short distance, opposite a white house with its name "Quinta" on the fence, and before the entry sign to Keswick, go up some steps in the grass verge, cross the road with care and take the public footpath "Crosthwaite Church" to the left of the house. Follow the path a short distance to return to St Kentigern's Church and the end of the walk.

Walk 3(b), Crosthwaite only: 5 miles

Follow Walk 3(a) to the lay-by near Chestnut Cottage **(D)**. Then continue along the minor road for a further 800 metres to reach the A591 Keswick-Carlisle road. Cross the road with caution, turn left and return to Crosthwaite from **(I)** as described above.

Walk 3(c), St Bega only: 6 miles

Park the car in the lay-by near Chestnut Cottage and continue from **(D)** as described in Walk 3(a) above. When you reach the minor road signposted "Millbeck, Applethwaite, Skiddaw" at **(I)**, turn left along this road which will bring you back to the lay-by and the end of the walk.

Walk 4: Ennerdale Bridge
Siblings, Stowbank and shore of lake

Location: St Mary's Church (NY068158) is in Ennerdale Bridge, 11 miles from Cockermouth, off the A5086 Cockermouth to Egremont road.

Distance: 7 miles (or 3 miles with a short cut).

Map: OS Outdoor Leisure 4: The English Lakes North Western area.

Terrain: This walk is mainly on footpaths across fields and along farm tracks with a small amount on very quiet country lanes. Walking is mainly on the level, although at the early stages there is a gradual pull up from the valley.

Church: St Mary, Ennerdale Bridge.

Car parking: There is parking on the lane outside the church. Approaching Ennerdale Bridge from Cockermouth, go through the village and turn immediately right at the children's playground onto the lane that leads to the church.

The Church

Here is a beautifully located church hidden amid trees in a quiet corner of the village with the River Ehen visible on the north side and the Fox and Hounds pub just around the corner. It is nice to find a welcome in several foreign languages on the noticeboard by the entrance to the churchyard. A chapel appears to have stood on this site since at least the early 16th century, when the Abbot of St Bees granted burial rights at Ennerdale. Several hundred years later it was known by Wordsworth, who in his poem, *The Brothers*, written in 1800, refers to "the homely priest of Ennerdale".

The present church, however, was built in 1856-8 and, as the builders of that time often liked to incorporate Norman features into their work, you will be met by a Norman style arched entrance, although thereafter the church has no pretensions to being other than of the Victorian era. Nevertheless, it has none of the excesses often associated with that period and there is a notable absence of wall adornments. It is more like a simple dales church: plain white walls, neat and well cared for. The light pine pews

Norman-style entrance to St Mary, Ennerdale Bridge

still preserve their umbrella stands with brass brackets and porcelain bases. It has a single chamber with a high roof, which gives a sense of light and spaciousness. The carpeted aisle leads to the plain altar in the very small arched chancel, which is believed to contain some genuine Norman stones. The west wall of the church is graced by two stained glass windows with attractive pale-coloured petal motifs and, at the time of writing, plans for creating a new meeting room at this end of the church were on display.

Among the other features of interest are:

❖ A tablet on the wall behind the pulpit in memory of "generous benefactors", Joseph Charters Brown and his wife Sarah Jane. The stained glass windows behind the altar are also in memory of the Browns.

❖ A stone tablet on the wall to the right of the organ, which commemorates a vicar who served many years in the earlier chapel on this site.

❖ Parishioners from this remote corner obviously travelled far afield in the 19th century. A substantial, but somewhat damaged and worn, monument behind iron railings in the north-east of the churchyard is in memory of two sons of a former vicar who were interred in foreign fields.

❖ Two other travellers, seafarers by profession, are remembered in the south-west of the graveyard.

Information available in the church:

❶ A leaflet, *The Parish of Lamplugh with Ennerdale.*

The Walk

Leave St Mary's churchyard **(A)** and turn right to cross the bridge over a stream. Turn immediately right at the footpath sign and proceed about twenty metres with a row of white washed cottages on your left, to pass through a kissing gate into a field. Then follow the path round two sides of the field, along the bank of the River Ehen, with a wire fence on your right. About a hundred metres before the end of the field cross over a stile on your right and bear left to follow the river downstream a short way and cross the river by a wooden footbridge at a footpath sign. Turn left and continue downstream to reach some duck boarding and a stile at the edge of a wood.

In the wood bear right to climb through the trees steeply for a short distance. The path bends left to a waymark sign, almost at the top of the rise, and you continue heading left in the direction indicated, to reach a stile in a fence in an old hedgerow. Cross two further stiles in very quick succession to enter a field on your right. Take care not to descend at this point, but continue straight ahead with a fence and an old hedgerow on your right. Now you should be able to see a quarry on the horizon ahead. At the end of the field cross over a stile and turn left to cross another stile. Turn right and proceed along the field edge in the same direction with the hedge on your right. Cross over a waymarked stile next to a gate and go straight over the field towards the farm buildings ahead, to cross a further stile next to a gate at a public footpath sign **(B)**.

Turn right along the metalled country lane. Then after about 200 metres turn right and cross a stile next to a cattle grid to follow the public footpath "High Stowbank via Stockhow" along a clear track. Continue along this track for about 500 metres as it bears between the farm buildings of Stockhow Hall and goes in front of the farmhouse before passing through a metal gate next to a waymark sign **(C)**.

Continue over the field ahead keeping to the left to cross a stile next to a gate. Cross over the next field with a fence and hedgerow on your right to go over a beck by means of some duck boarding and cross a waymarked stile. Now climb a short way and proceed ahead, keeping the trees on your left, to leave the field by a stile next to a metal gate. Cross the track and immediately take another stile next to a gate to meet the road near High Stowbank farm **(D)**.

(Those wishing to take a short cut and return to Ennerdale Bridge at this point should turn right and follow the road for about a mile back to the village and St Mary's Church).

To continue, cross over the road and follow the public footpath "Croasdale via Hunter How ". The path, however, is really a lane which you follow to Bankend Cottages **(E)**. Just past the cottages, leave the lane via a stile to follow a public footpath on your right for "Croasdale via Hunter How". Proceed in the direction of the signpost to go through a waymarked metal gate. Bear left towards a marshy area to cross a stile in the old hedgerow and immediately another waymarked stile and then a footbridge over a stream. Proceed straight ahead towards the dwellings in the opposite corner, negotiating the marshy land as best as possible, and cross a footbridge. Then cross a stile next to a gate and go through a waymarked gate at Hunter How farm **(F)**.

Turn right along the farm track to go through a gate and over a stile next to a metal gate near the farm buildings. Now take care here to keep to the right and close to the fence on your right, as the main farm track forks to the left. If you have taken care, you will spot a waymarked stile next to gate on your right. Once over the stile follow the path ahead as it winds down to another waymarked stile next to a gate and then crosses a small beck. Make for a stone post by some trees about 100 metres or so ahead. Follow the line of the fence and the old hedgerow on your right to reach the bottom of the field and cross a kissing gate and a narrow footbridge. Now you just need to climb a ladder stile a few metres ahead next to a gate to join the lane and pause for breath! Cross over the lane and the stile opposite and follow the direction of the public footpath sign up the field to a stile in the far left-hand corner of the field. Cross the stile, bear right through a gateway and continue ahead with the fence on your left, climbing steadily for some 250 metres to a waymarked wooden gate. After about 10 more metres, turn left through a gap in the broken wall and then immediately right to follow the line of old hedgerow up towards a public footpath sign. Exit via a stile onto the lane, just below the farm buildings of Howside amid the trees **(G)**.

Turn right and continue for some 400 metres down to a junction at which you turn left. Walk along the road and after a further few hundred metres look out for a view of Ennerdale Water. Soon a road sign and a public footpath sign will direct you along a metalled farm lane towards the lake 800 metres further on. The lane passes to the right of How Hall Farm **(H)**.

Take the stile next to a gate at a National Trust notice to follow a track down towards the lake and through a kissing gate to the lakeside **(I)**.

Turn right and simply follow the lakeside over the stiles and through the gates. Enjoy the splendid views across the lake as you continue as far as the weir at the end of the lake **(J)**.

Cross over the weir by the footbridge, turn right to leave the lake and walk along the broad track, ignoring the fork to the right by a cairn. Go through the kissing gate and at the entrance to the public car park turn left on the metalled road to pass Bleach Green Cottages on your right. Go through a gate next to a cattle grid and head towards the wood. Then bear right on the clear track to go through a gate and join another track at the edge of a wood. Turn right and walk along the broad track with a wall on your right. At the end of the wall, take the green track on your right, following the wall down towards a wood. Cross over the waymarked stile next to a gate and in a short distance climb some stone steps to cross the River Ehen again over a gated footbridge. Continue ahead, take the stile by the old mill and bear left up the track past Grike cottage to meet the road at a corner **(K)**.

Bear left up the road, passing Braemar Cottages, to arrive at a T-junction **(L)**. Turn left and walk along this road for about 800 metres to reach Ennerdale Bridge. At the junction with the Cockermouth road, turn left to cross the bridge and then immediately right for the church and the end of the walk.

Walk 5: Grange-in-Borrowdale and Newlands

Dogtooth? Catbells and a Hedgehog Tale.

Location: Holy Trinity Church, Grange (NY253175) is in Grange-in-Borrowdale, 5 miles south of Keswick, just off the B5289.

Distance: Walk 5(a), Grange and Newlands: 8½ miles; Walk 5(b), Grange only: 3 miles; Walk 5(c), Newlands only: 3 miles.

Map: OS Outdoor Leisure 4: The English Lakes North Western area.

Terrain: All three walks are almost entirely on public footpaths. Walk 5(a) has a long climb with some steep sections. Walks 5(b) and 5(c) are mainly on the level.

Churches: Holy Trinity, Grange; Grange Methodist Church; Newlands Church.

Car parking: There is limited parking outside Holy Trinity Church and Grange Methodist Church and in Grange itself. For Walk 5(c), there is parking at Chapel Bridge near Newlands Church (NY230194).

The Churches
Holy Trinity, Grange-in-Borrowdale

This church was built in 1860 at the behest of Miss Margaret Heathcote of Borrowdale Gates whose photograph is in the church porch. She was quite a remarkable woman and her fascinating story is told in the leaflet referred to below.

It is small and compact as befits its location. A plaque in the porch indicates that the bell, given in memory of Thomas Threlkeld, is in fact too heavy to ring! The exterior is of Lakeland slate, as is that of the nearby Methodist church, however the interior, as might be expected, is a little more ornate than that of its neighbour. It is characterised by a jagged motif in the roof beams and the outside arches of the window. This appears to provide a fore-taste of the "jaws" of Borrowdale to the south and perhaps it is this rather raw appearance which may have caused Nikolaus Pevsner (*The Buildings of England: Cumberland and Westmorland*) to state that "the architect must have been an aggressive man". However, the overall effect is pleasant and positive. The absence of stained glass windows makes the church light and airy and helps to blend the interior with the surrounding countryside.

Among the other features of interest are:

❖ The cross of nails on the wall facing you in the tiny entrance room.

❖ The slate font at the west end.

❖ The panels on the east walls with the ten commandments painted by Margaret Heathcote, the church's founder.

❖ The simple wooden chairs on either side of the sanctuary.

Information available in the church:

❶ *The Parish of Borrowdale with Grange*, Revd T. Lowther (revised by Revd R. Johns).

The unusual interior of Holy Trinity, Grange-in-Borrowdale
(with the kind permission of the vicar)

Grange Methodist Church

This little chapel is delightfully positioned by a bridge over the River Derwent at the eastern entrance to this popular village. It provides a quiet oasis from the hustle and bustle of the tourist traffic and a genuine welcome to the passer-by.

Two stone slabs set in the Lakeland slate above the doorway proclaim the facts that the Wesleyan Chapel dates from 1894 and that the stone was laid by Joseph Threlkeld. There is a single plaque inside in memory of the same Joseph Threlkeld, "a devout worshipper and a generous benefactor". Otherwise, the interior is plain and simple in accordance with the Methodist tradition. It is a fine place to pause and reflect at the beginning or end of a journey.

Newlands Church

This beautiful little church, which has no dedication, stands in splendid isolation in the Newlands Valley and offers an immediate welcome in the words on the notice on the church door: "Whether you are exploring, have come for a few moments of prayer and meditation or are merely sheltering from the rain – We Welcome You". This is indeed a pleasant haven and perhaps a welcome respite after the walk from Grange, offering a chance to re-charge the batteries before the return journey. It is light, neat and relatively unadorned.

It is believed that there has been a chapel here from at least 1576, but this fell into such a poor state of repair that it needed rebuilding and renovating

Newlands Church

between 1843 and 1885. The small entrance porch has a low ceiling, with stairs off to the gallery, and doorways to the schoolroom and the vestry which contains some interesting old photographs. Inside, the church consists of a simple single chamber. The year 2000 saw the redecoration of the church and the addition of new lighting and heating. At the same time the adjoining schoolroom, which was in active use until 1967, was restored, refurbished, and dedicated by the Bishop of Carlisle as "a place of quiet and reflection". It now also offers "Newlands Teas" on summer Sunday afternoons!

Among the other features of interest are:

❖ The pleasant, if crudely carved, oak pulpit and the reading desk dated 1610.

❖ Two poignant reminders of the effect of wars on a small community: the window in the south wall and the tablet on the north wall.

❖ The coat of arms of George II, dated 1737, on the south wall.

❖ The notice/prayer board on the west wall given by a parish in Brazil.

Information available in the church:

❶ *Newlands – about this church*, Campbell Matthews (adapted from *A Quiet Corner of Lakeland* by George Bott).

The Walks

Walk 5(a), Grange and Newlands: 8½ miles

After visiting the churches (Grange Methodist Church **(B)** is beside the bridge over the River Derwent, about 200 metres east of Holy Trinity Church) take the public bridleway, "Honister, Rosthwaite, Seatoller" opposite Holy Trinity Church **(A)**, between the café and the Penny Brigg Guesthouse. After about 70 metres you will notice a cottage on your left which was given to the National Trust in memory of Joseph and Margaret Threlkeld, a further sign of the significance of this family in Grange. Continue along the metalled road and through a gate by a National Trust sign, ignoring paths and tracks to the left, until you reach Hollow Farm **(C)**.

Pass between the farm buildings bearing right to pass through a kissing gate next to the farm gate. Continue ahead to go through a gate under the trees. Turn right and follow the track until eventually you reach a stone wall in front of a wood. Turn left and walk ahead to the right of a small low footpath sign, keeping the wall and the wood close on your right. At the top of the rise, you will pass a neatly enclosed sewage works and here you should bear right to pass over a stile in the fence and then continue bearing right round the edge of the wood. Cross the stream at the most convenient spot and pick up a path descending to the right and skirting the wood. There are a number of paths in more or less the same direction, but you should keep relatively close to the wood. Continue in the same direction until eventually a house appears ahead and you come to a sign "Permitted footpath Catbells-Newlands". Take the permitted footpath and skirt the wood ahead to proceed with the fence on your right until you meet a track, with a gate and a stile on your right **(D)**.

Do not cross the stile, but instead, turn left up this very popular "highway" leading up towards Catbells. This is a well-trodden steady climb. Keep to the main path, ignoring any tempting ones off to the right. Stop from time to time to catch your breath and admire the views over Derwentwater as the whole lake gradually comes into view and you can see Keswick and Skiddaw to the north and Grange and Castle Crag to the south. The National Trust have worked hard to prevent erosion and several well-stepped stone sections are a great help. After at least one false summit you eventually reach Hause Gate and meet another popular track for those doing the ridge walk **(E)**.

Turn left, follow the track for about 200 metres and, just as the track becomes stony, take the faint path off to the right to begin your descent into Newlands Valley. As the path forks, bear left to pass a sheepfold on your left and then follow a series of cairns, picking your way across the scree and crossing a stream. As the path takes you around the base of Looking Crag you will see the chimney pots of Littletown in the hollow ahead. In a short distance, you will meet a clear track on the right coming from Skelgill **(F)**.

Skelgill and the area behind Catbells is associated with Beatrix Potter's tale of Lucie and the hedgehog, Mrs Tiggy-Winkle. The story was dedicated to the real Lucie, daughter of the Vicar of Newlands, your next church.

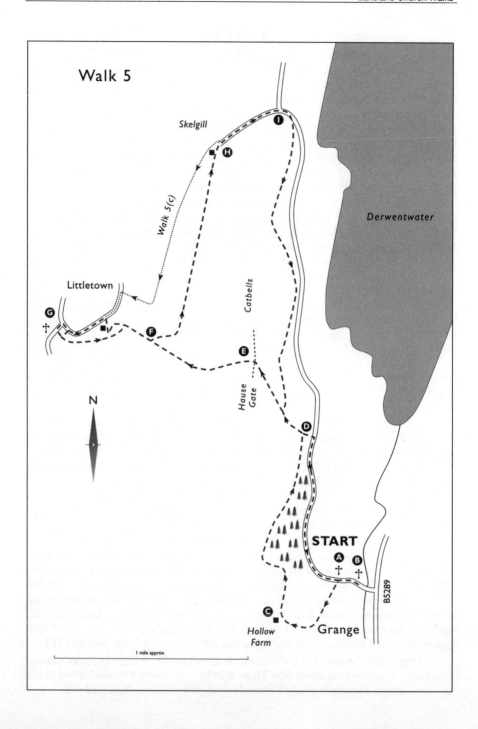

Walk 5

Skelgill

Walk 5(c)

Littletown

Derwentwater

Catbells

Hause Gate

N

START

Hollow Farm

Grange

B5289

1 mile approx

Bear left at the junction of paths and proceed along the clear track with a wall on your right and continue on the same track as it winds past a cottage and goes through a gate onto a country lane at the south end of Littletown. Turn left, walk down the road for about 400 metres to cross Chapel Bridge and then turn left through the gateway to follow the sign to Newlands Church **(G)**.

After visiting Newlands Church, retrace your steps back over Chapel Bridge. About 100 metres beyond the car parking area, leave the road on the right and climb a short way, past a "no parking" sign, to take a stile onto a stepped path. Go straight up the path and after a few metres at a junction turn right. Proceed on the track for about 100 metres and then take a sharp turn to the left to double back on a green track. Follow the track for a few hundred metres until you meet the stony track, down which you descended on your way to meet the road at Littletown. Bear right and follow the track as it ascends, keeping the wall on your left to arrive at the junction where you came down from Hause Gate **(F)**.

Bear left and proceed through the old quarry, bearing right to cross the narrow bridge over the stream. Now with Catbells above you on the right, continue along a pleasant track as the end of Bassenthwaite Lake gradually comes into sight. The path eventually descends to meet a metalled farm track at Skelgill farm **(H)**.

Bear right along the metalled farm track until it joins a road at a bend **(I)**. Resist the temptation to go left towards Portinscale and Keswick and instead bear right along the road for about 150 metres to pick up a bridlepath on the right. Now climb gradually parallel to the road taking time to admire the views of Derwentwater as the full length of the lake gradually comes into view. Now you have nothing to worry about as the broad path follows the contours of Catbells above and the road below. At one point you briefly descend to the road in order to circumnavigate an old quarry before ascending again You will soon have a good opportunity for a rest on the fine stone seat erected in memory of Sir Hugh Walpole, overlooking his former home, Brackenburn.

> *Hugh Walpole (1884-1941) purchased Brackenburn in 1923 and used it as a regular retreat from his London residence. Here he enjoyed the peace and quiet in which he could pursue his prolific career as a novelist. The Lake District inspired him to write The Herries Chronicle, a saga of 18th-century life in this area. A churchgoing man, he attended Holy Trinity Church, Grange on occasions, but worshipped more frequently at St John's in Keswick where he is buried.*

Now continue ahead keeping the stone wall and the wood on your left until you meet the "highway" you took earlier up towards Catbells. Turn left and go down the track to the stile next to a gate **(D)**.

Cross the stile, descend to the minor road and turn right. Now walk along the road for about 800 metres admiring the views of the "Jaws of Borrowdale" ahead. You pass the Borrowdale Gates Hotel, originally the home of Margaret Heathcote, founder of Holy Trinity Church and then the old school, where a plaque commemorates this same lady, before arriving back at Grange and the end of the walk.

Walk 5(b), Grange only: 3 miles

Follow Walk 5(a), as described above, as far as **(D)**. Then exit via the stile next to the gate onto the quiet country road. Turn right and walk back to Grange enjoying the sights described at the end of Walk 5(a).

Walk 5(c), Newlands only: 3 miles

After visiting Newlands Church, follow Walk 5(a), as described above, from **(G)** to **(H)**. To return to Newlands, turn left and go through the gate into Skelgill farm. Descend a few metres and turn left by the right-hand side of the farmhouse to follow the partially concealed public footpath sign. Pass through the gate onto the clear path beyond. Continue straight ahead across the fields by a series of stiles/gates to eventually take a ladder stile next to a gate. Follow the green path for about 70 metres as it bears slightly left along the line of the hedgerow on your left and then, just before the hedgerow ends, bear right to climb slightly and pass a broken wall some 80 metres further on. Continue on the faint green track with a hedgerow on the right to go through a kissing gate. Follow the grassy path as it gently descends. It crosses a small beck and the track becomes more obvious. Take time to appreciate the contours of the hills surrounding the Newlands Valley. You will see the old quarry ahead to the left. Continue on the clear track ahead via a series of stiles/gates until you reach a metalled lane by a sign, "Public Bridleway leading to Catbells footpath and Hause Gate". Turn left and walk along the lane passing Littletown Farm and the neighbouring cottages before descending quite steeply to the car park by Chapel Bridge and the end of the walk.

Walk 6: Isel and Bridekirk
Fonts, footpaths and fast flowing river

Location: St Michael's Church (NY162333) is located 3 miles from Cockermouth on a minor road which crosses the River Derwent at Isel Bridge.

Distance: Walk 6(a), Isel and Bridekirk including Sunderland: 13 miles; Walk 6(b), Isel and Bridekirk only: 10 miles; Walk 6(c), Isel only: 5½ miles.

Map: OS Outdoor Leisure 4: The English Lakes North Western area.

Terrain: The three walks are largely on public footpaths across fields with some sections on minor roads. Walks 6(a) and (b) involve some gradual climbs and a visit to Cockermouth. Walk 6(c) is mainly on the level.

Churches: St Michael, Isel; St Bridget, Bridekirk

Car parking: Parking is available at St Michael.

The Churches
St Michael, Isel

Several meanings have been suggested for the name "Isel" but that favoured by the church booklet, "Isa's flat land within the bend of the river", seems the most appropriate for the peaceful situation by the River Derwent. Apart from the former vicarage, the church is the only building and, set in its quiet churchyard backed by trees and overlooking green fields, there is an overall feeling of tranquillity here. Sir John Betjeman (*Guide to English Parish Churches*) ranked Isel as, "a perfect English harmony of man and nature".

There was probably an earlier church on the site but the present building dates from about 1130. It retains its Norman appearance – a small low structure with narrow windows and a lower chancel roof – and the stonework of the north and south walls, the south doorway and the chancel arch is Norman. Some of the roof trusses may also date from that period. A defen-

St Michael, Isel

sive tower, common for border churches, was built onto the west end. The date of its construction is not known but it existed in 1710 and was demolished sometime thereafter, being replaced by the small bellcote. An extensive restoration programme in 1878 was essentially just that – i.e. restoration with little additional Victorian embellishment apart from the west window.

Norman landowners of Isel included the Engaynes (see Walk 12, St Cuthbert's, Clifton) who married into the Morville family. As a result of Hugh Morville's part in the assassination of Archbishop Becket in 1170, Isel parish was forfeited to the crown and was placed under the care of Hexham Abbey. It was restored to the lords of Isel by Elizabeth I. First the Leighs and then the Lawson family succeeded to the Lordship of Isel.

Entry is through the 14th-century porch and the Norman doorway, which has similar pillar decorations as those on the chancel arch. Inside, the nave, with the pews from 1878, leads through the Norman arch into the extended chancel. There are quite a few wall plaques commemorating members of local families – in particular the Lawsons (see below, Isel Hall).

The church retains many interesting features, some of which are listed below. Sadly, over the last couple of decades several important items have been stolen, including the Triskele Stone, a part of a 10th-century cross shaft. It is perhaps more in sorrow than in anger that the author of the church guidebook has to report "As a security measure nothing worth stealing is kept in the church nowadays".

Among the other features of interest are:

❖ Inside the porch on the right-hand side of the Norman doorway, a sundial cut into one of the stones. The dial includes times of some of the services said by the clergy and other times which might refer to when children attended school there. An explanation is on the south wall near the font.

❖ The octagonal stone font dated about 1275. Although now with plain sides, it has been suggested that it might have had similar carvings as the Bridekirk font.

❖ The pulpit made in 1878 from the old oak furnishings.

❖ The unusual stepped window sill near the pulpit. No firm conclusions as to its origin and purpose have been reached. A set of explanatory notes is kept on the window sill.

❖ The attractive overhead wrought iron lamp holders for the paraffin lamps.

Information available in the church:

❶ _St Michael's Church Isel Cumbria: A Brief History_, W. Raymond Hartland.

St Bridget, Bridekirk

The church of St Bridget stands hidden behind the churchyard trees, at the northern end of the village of Bridekirk, with splendid views over rolling countryside towards the distant Galloway Hills. Although the church is not usually open, other than for weekly services, details of how to gain admission are posted on the south-east door. However, there is still a lot to see here.

After passing through the lych-gate, inscribed, "Enter into His gates with thanksgiving", you find the ruined chancel walls of a church built in 1130, probably on the site of an earlier wooden one. This Norman church fell into such a poor state of repair that in 1868 it was felt it needed to be demolished and completely replaced. Apparently, there were insufficient funds to remove the chancel walls and so they remain today as testimony to the early history of the parish. Within the pleasant old walls there are some 19th-century memorials including a metal plaque recalling a child who died the day he was born in 1805.

The old chancel walls are not the only surviving remains of St Bridget's long history. Even without enterinpg the "new" church, we can see a fine collection of grave slabs standing against its outside walls. The small south-east doorway is from the earlier church and to the left of it, set into the wall, is a medieval stone on which are carved a heart, hands and feet, thought to depict the wounds of Christ. Inside there are two arches from the old church and several other features of interest which are detailed in the church guidebook.

The most outstanding feature of the church is undoubtedly the mid-12th-century baptismal font, described by Nikolaus Pevsner (*The Buildings of England: Cumberland and Westmorland*) as "...one of the liveliest pieces of Norman sculpture in the county...exceptional". The splendidly decorated panels include carvings of grotesque animals and foliage, as well as depictions of the Baptism of Christ and the expulsion of Adam and Eve

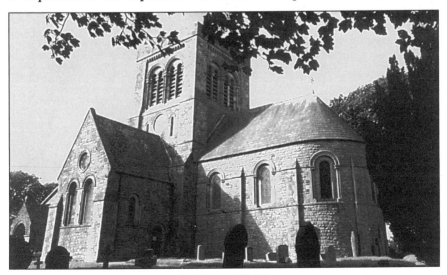

St Bridget, Bridekirk

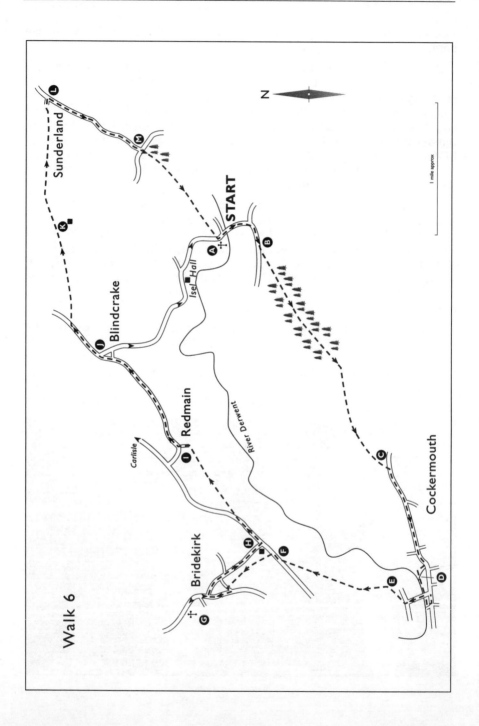

Walk 6

from the Garden of Eden. The sculptor, said to be Richard of Durham, shows himself at work on his masterpiece.

Information available in the church:

❶ Hand-held information board.

❶ *Historical Notes on Bridekirk Parish Church*, Revd Ernest Rogers, with additional notes.

The Walks

Walk 6(a), Isel and Bridekirk including Sunderland: 13 miles

Leave St Michael's Church (A), walk back up the church drive to the road and turn right. Follow the road as it passes Isel Bridge House and bears right to cross the bridge over the River Derwent. The road now climbs quite steeply to a T-junction. Turn right in the direction of Cockermouth. Continue for about 250 metres, ignoring the gateway on the left to Setmurthy Common, and as the road bears right leave it to take a public bridleway on the left which is part of the Allerdale Ramble and the Reivers Off Road route (B).

Go through the gate and follow the clear track, as it gradually climbs. Eventually, after ascending through the trees for some time, you reach a break in the trees of about 100 metres and you come to a fork in the track. Take the right fork ("Reivers Off Road") and climb through the edge of the wood up the broad stony track. As the track begins to go off to the left, bear right to leave the wood via a stile next to a gate. Continue ahead on the grassy track with a wall on your right. Soon after passing the corner of the wall and ignoring a waymarked gate, you begin to get splendid views of Cockermouth below with the spire of All Saints Church (1852) where Wordsworth's father is buried. Continue downhill with the wall on your right via several gates/stiles until the path eventually bears left to exit onto a road (C).

Turn right and follow the paved path by the roadside passing Cockermouth High School. A few hundred metres after the school you cross Isel Road and about 100 metres further on you pass the remains of the 14th-century Cockermouth Castle (now a private residence with largely Victorian additions). Just beyond the castle, turn right at the Quince and Medlar (a noted vegetarian restaurant) and descend to pass Jennings' Brewery (1828). Continue ahead to cross a bridge over the River Cocker just prior to its confluence with the River Derwent (D).

Turn right and go along Waterloo Street for a few hundred metres and turn right opposite River View to follow the sign "To the river". Go along the riverside path and a few metres after passing beneath a footbridge you pass the walled garden of Wordsworth House, birthplace of the poet William Wordsworth.

William Wordsworth was born in 1770 in Cockermouth in the large house which his father occupied as a result of working as an agent for Sir James Lowther. William's mother died when he was eight and, after a short period in Penrith with his grandparents, he was sent to school in Hawkshead from

1779 to 1787 and there he attended St Michael's Church (see Walk 28). After University at Cambridge and travels in England and Europe, he returned to the Lake District in 1800 and settled in Grasmere. During the next 50 years, he and his literary friends established the Lake District as a major centre of creative writing. Wordsworth included many references to Lakeland churches in his works (see, for example, Walk 16, Wythburn) and he was also a good walker, capable of doing 30 miles in a day to visit friends. He died in 1850 and he is remembered in Grasmere Church (see Walk 27) and Ambleside Church (see Walk 29).

The path turns left into a side road that soon leads to Main Street. Turn left and pass in front of Wordsworth House. Continue for some 40 metres and then turn first left down Bridge St. Go over the footbridge and keep straight ahead to pass the former Derwent Mill, now converted into apartments. Go over the road junction and follow the pavement as it bears right. Cross over the road to follow a public footpath sign before the Cumbria County Council buildings and follow the path with a wall/hedge on your left to a stone stile next to a gate to the left of a cattle pen **(E)**.

Cross the stile and bear slightly left as you climb the steep grassy bank ahead. Continue ahead to go through a metal kissing gate and the small metal gate behind. Walk straight ahead over the pasture land, climbing gradually more or less parallel to the telegraph wires on your left. Then, at the top of the rise, make for the large stone stile in the right-hand corner of the hedge. Cross the stile and bear right with a hedge/wire fence on your right to cross another large stone stile. Proceed in the same direction up the side of the next field with a plantation on your right to cross a further stone stile next to a gate. The path levels off as you continue ahead with the wire fence on your right and then drops down to a driveway (to Wood Hall). Cross the driveway in the direction of the public footpath sign. The path is rather vague as you climb to the left of the hawthorn bushes and pass a clump of trees to reach a waymarked stile at the corner of a plantation. Cross the stile and proceed in the direction of the waymark along the top of the ridge to a stone stile. Cross the stile to exit onto the A595 Cockermouth-Carlisle road **(F)**.

Turn right and walk along the wide grass verge for some 275 metres before crossing the busy road with care to find a slightly concealed public footpath sign "Bridekirk ½" just beyond a telegraph pole. Go through the gap in the wall and over a stile. Bear slightly right to cross the field in the direction of the sign towards a telegraph pole. Continue straight ahead past the telegraph pole and cross a stone stile. Continue along the side of the next field with a wall on your right. As the wall turns to the right proceed straight ahead and follow the line of old trees to meet a wooden fence. Follow the footpath diversion sign for a few metres to take a wooden and a stone stile onto a minor road. Turn left and after about 60 metres at a junction turn right passing Bonny Hill Farm on your left. Continue for a few hundred metres to reach a junction by Low Road Cottage. Turn left and walk down the road past the junction with the Dovenby-Maryport road to arrive soon at St Bridget's Church **(G)**.

After visiting the old chancel, the church grounds and possibly the church, retrace your steps back up the road to the fork at Low Road Cottage. Keep to the left fork (not the road you came down) to walk past some fine properties and past the junction with a road off to the right. As the road bears left, continue straight ahead onto a narrow lane. Follow the lane and ahead in the distance you may see Skiddaw. After a few hundred metres you rejoin the Cockermouth-Carlisle road by Sundawn (H).

Again cross the road with care, turn left and walk along the generous grass verge for about 400 metres to a lay-by. Go over the stile next to the gate and take the public footpath "Redmain". Bear diagonally left across the corner of the field to take a stile. Continue straight ahead across the field and make for the left-hand side of the plantation ahead. Then continue with the edge of the wood on your right to cross a stile. Continue in the same direction along the side of the wood and after some 300 metres cross another stile at the corner of the wood. Walk towards the rocky outcrop ahead, behind in the distance is Binsey the Lake District's most northerly fell. Just before the rocky outcrop a clear track goes off to the left, follow it as it descends to join another track. Continue straight ahead and soon pass through a gate by Redmain Gill. Follow the metalled road past the farm buildings and climb a short distance to join a minor road (I).

Turn right and proceed through the small hamlet of Redmain. You need to follow this quiet road for a mile to Blindcrake. After several hundred metres there are excellent views on your right of Isel Hall (see below) with glimpses of the River Derwent. As you enter Blindcrake ignore the first road off to the right to Isel and continue ahead for a short distance to come to a junction with a signpost pointing to Isel (there is a telephone box on the opposite corner) (J).

Proceed straight ahead for about 500 metres with some interesting properties on your left and just before the last dwelling look for a fingerpost on the right "Public Footpath Sunderland 2 miles". Walk up the broad track between the trees crossing a stile next to a gate. A waymarked ladder stile takes you into a field. Now continue straight on and, as you climb, a stone wall appears ahead. Make for the left-hand corner and when you reach it, stop to admire the views. Follow the line of the wall, keeping the wall on your right. Carry straight on past a wire fence which goes protectively around a rocky dip and descend to pick up a broad green path which lies ahead. Walk in the direction of the small plantation on top of the crags and when you reach a vehicular track turn right and follow it for about 75 metres. Leave the track and make for the right-hand corner of the crags. Shortly you need to follow another vehicular track down towards a waymarked metal gate. Do not go through this gate but bear left to walk ahead with the fence on your right and follow the path as it skirts the crags immediately above. Over the field on your right is a ruined farmhouse (K).

The path crosses two ladder stiles near to each other. Now walk across the field keeping close to the trees on your left until you reach a stile next to a metal gate. Ahead to the right you may see the buildings of your next destination, Sunderland. Cross the stile and proceed ahead towards the boundary wall bearing slightly right to reach the corner of a fence and another wall. A few metres before the boundary wall, go through a gate on your right beside a waymark post. Turn left and proceed with a fence on your right to follow the stony path as it descends between two lines of trees to a gate. Go through the gate and make for a stile next to a gate in the stone wall about 75 metres ahead. Take the stile and cross the field to pass between two stone gateposts next to a stile. The path now descends on an old track, passing further old stone gateposts, to reach a farm track. Turn left and go though the gateway. Continue down the track ignoring a track off to the left, to arrive at a metalled road. Turn left and after a few metres turn right at a T-junction in the pleasant hamlet of Sunderland **(L)**.

Now walk along this quiet road for about a mile, passing Linskeldfield Farm on your left, until you arrive at another T-junction **(M)**.

Cross the stile opposite, next to a gate, and follow the public footpath sign over the field with a wood on your left; this section can be very muddy. Cross the stream by the footbridge, climb up the bank and continue in the same direction over the next field with a wire fence on your left. Take the stile next to two metal gates and proceed across the field with a wire fence now on your right. Go over another stile next to a metal gate and continue along the clear track until you reach a metal gate marked "Private". Take the stile on your right next to a wooden gate, ignore the public bridleway directions, and walk diagonally left for about 50 metres to cross a further stile. Go over the plank bridge and cross a stile. Now continue straight ahead with a wire fence on your left, crossing a stile and finally exiting via a gate onto the road opposite the church and the end of the walk

Walk 6(b), Isel and Bridekirk only: 10 miles
Follow Walk 6(a) as far as **(J)**. At this point turn right in the direction of the signpost for Isel, walk down the road for just over a mile to pass Isel Hall (see below) and return to Isel church and the end of the walk.

Walk 6(c), Isel only: 5½ miles
After visiting the church **(A)**, walk back up the church drive to the road and turn left. Walk along this quiet minor road and ahead you will glimpse Isel Hall between the trees with the River Derwent below. Follow the road for about a mile, passing the fine properties of The Old Almshouses on your right and then Isel Hall on your left.

> *Isel Hall was the home of the Lawson family, in direct and indirect line for some 400 years. Not surprisingly, therefore, the family is well remembered in Isel church. You may notice a crest on the stone gateway with two arms of the law supporting a sun, an ornamental pun on the name Lawson!*

After passing The Old School the road begins to climb a little more steeply, and eventually passes through Blindcrake to arrive at a T-junction with a telephone box on the right. Turn right and continue as for Walk 6(a) from **(J)**.

ιι. ͻ⁻ · ο ͼ

Walk 7: Loweswater
Farmsteads, fells and forest

Location: St Bartholomew's Church (NY141209) is in the small hamlet of Loweswater, which is located between Loweswater and Crummock Water. It is a few hundred metres off the minor road that links the B5289 with the A5086. It is near the Kirkstile Inn, which is signposted from the minor road.

Distance: Walk 7(a), Loweswater Church, Crummock Water and Loweswater: 6½ miles. Walk 7(b), Loweswater Church and Crummock Water: 2½ miles. Walk 7(c), Maggie's Bridge, Holme Wood and Loweswater: 4½ miles.

Map: OS Outdoor Leisure 4: The English Lakes North Western area.

Terrain: Walks 7(a) and 7(c) are mainly on public footpaths and forest tracks with one long gradual ascent. Walk 7(b) is mainly on public footpaths and is on the level.

Church: St Bartholomew, Loweswater.

Car parking: There is a small car parking area about 100 metres below the church over the bridge to the right. Parking is available at the Kirkstile Inn opposite the church for genuine patrons. There is a National Trust car park at Maggie's Bridge near Loweswater 800 metres to the west of the church; this can be used as an alternative starting point for Walks 7(a) and 7(c).

The Church

This is a single chamber church, with a bellcote at the west end, together with an apse and tiny transepts at the east end. As a building, it is neither more nor less attractive than many similar churches but its situation is superb. There have been earlier churches here or close by; records of St Bees Priory include reference to a place of worship at Loweswater in 1125. The origins of the present building date back to 1829 when a new church was consecrated. The simple chapel built then was restored and enlarged in 1884. Nikolaus Pevsner (*The Buildings of England: Cumberland and Westmoreland*) considers that most of what is now seen appears to be from that time, with the possible exception of the nave windows.

On entering the church through the porch at the north-west corner there is a sense, like that of Dr Who's Tardis, of its being much larger inside than the impression gained from outside. Indeed, with its extensive rows of pews and choir stalls, it is a big church for the scattered community of Loweswater. Received local wisdom is that it owes its size to the decision to rebuild in 1884. This was made in the anticipation of there being a large increase in population because of a proposed lead mining venture. The church was rebuilt but the venture did not live up to expectations.

Internally, there is a nave with exposed roof beams leading to the chancel in the apse. Overall, there is a feeling of simplicity. This is possibly underlined by the absence of stained glass, apart from the attractive red borders around the windows. The plain glass of the east window gives a view of the fells beyond and worshippers might well recall the words of Psalm 121 "I will lift up my eyes to the hills".

Furnishings include memorial tablets on the north and south walls and a

St Bartholomew, Loweswater, and neighbouring inn

list of incumbents. John Borranskail, the second incumbent, served in this place for 73 years! "Wonderful Walker" (see Walk 21, Seathwaite Church) had his first teaching appointment at Loweswater and while here was ordained to Holy Orders.

Loweswater has a long association with the schooling of local children – the first school house was built in 1780 and the school itself in the next year. A larger school built in 1832 continued until its closure in 1952; it is now the village hall. (The school house is now Rose Cottage and you pass this and the village hall on Walk 7(a); Walk 7(c) also passes the village hall).

Among the other features of interest are:

❖ The board, on the west wall, on which the Ten Commandments, Creed and Lord's Prayer are painted; the only surviving furniture from the 1829 church.

❖ The inscription on the lectern "In Memoriam 1914 - 1918" with five names.

❖ The dedication on the east window to Penelope Balogh, a distinguished psychotherapist and former wife of Lord Balogh, the economic adviser to Harold Wilson's government.

❖ The attractive kneelers, which include some local scenes and which were made by parishioners.

5

The Walks

rch, Crummock Water and Loweswater: 6½ miles

ıds, turn left and walk down the road for 100
rection of the "no through road" sign and pro-
ver the bridge and past two properties, one a
ther a modern glass fronted house. Over to
nock Water. Continue on the path, which
gate. Go through the gate and bear right to
here is a stone wall on your right and beyond
ıke. When you reach the end of the trees on
ın the left. Initially this doubles back behind
t. Follow the path as it skirts Raven Crag, on
vering above you on the right. The path bears
wall on your left. At the end of the wall carry
path as it bears to the left to descend towards
te and walk between the cottages, one on the
to exit onto a minor road **(B)**.

metres take the public footpath on your left. Initially you walk alongside Park Beck on your left. Go through a gate and follow the path as it bears right and the tip of Crummock Water comes into view. Cross a stile and carry on with a stone wall on your left and go over another stile. Follow the gravel path which crosses a small footbridge. Turn left onto the wooden boarding running across your path to walk the few metres to cross a stile, to the right of a stone wall. Bear left and walk ahead to cross a concrete bridge over a stream. Go through a gate and walk straight ahead to go almost immediately through another gate (marked "Private Road – footpath only"). You are now on a broad gravel path. Follow the path through a series of gates to exit onto a metalled road. Muncaster House is ahead **(C)**.

Walk past Muncaster House and immediately after the property, take the public footpath sign to go over a stile into a field. Loweswater Church is ahead over the fields. Bear left to walk along the field edge with a wire fence on your left. Go over a stile into the next field and carry on bearing slightly right across the field to arrive at a waymarked gate to the left of a ladder stile. Cross the stile and walk straight ahead to a gate near a small waymarked fingerpost. Go through the gate and walk past Gillerthwaite to exit onto a minor road. There is a telephone box over to the left **(D)**.

Turn up the road to the right of the telephone box, walk past Rose Cottage and the vicarage on your right, the road sign to Kirkstile Inn on your left, with the village hall on the corner **(E)**.

Proceed for about 400 metres and take the public footpath "Loweswater" on your left. Proceed down the narrow, metalled road. You might have to squeeze up to the hedge to allow clear passage to any cars you encounter. At the end of this road is Maggie's Bridge, where there is a National Trust car park on your right. This car park provides a suitable alternative as a starting point for the walk. To continue the walk do not go into the car park but take the track to the left before the car park entrance to come to a gateway **(F)**.

Go through the gate and follow the farm track, which is well-defined and gradually starts to climb towards High Nook farm, which can be seen ahead. This is one of those places where there are truly magnificent views all around you. Walk through the farmyard and after the gate at the end of the farm area bear left with a stone wall and then a fence on your left. Continue until reaching a gate in a stone wall, which marks the boundary of the National Trust land. Over to the right are the woods on the side of Carling Knott, which will be reached a little later on the walk. Go through the gate and carry straight on, ignoring the track going uphill on your left. In 300 metres or so you reach a point where the path divides **(G)**.

Take the right-hand fork and walk downhill to reach a plank bridge over Highnook Beck. Cross the bridge and follow the path uphill towards the wood ahead. The path goes to the left-hand corner of the edge of the wood; it is a long ascent up a grassy path. As you climb higher, take the opportunity to stop once or twice to look back. Below, you can see the whole of High Nook Tarn, whilst further away to the left, Crummock Water peeps out from behind Mellbreak. Keep walking uphill until the edge of the wood is reached **(H)**.

Follow the path with the wood on your right. There is a gradual climb with higher craggy ground on the left and glimpses of Loweswater through the trees on the right. Keep following the path as it skirts the wood and crosses a stile next to a gate. When the path nears the end of the wood, the countryside opens out to a splendid panoramic view with the Solway Firth and Scottish hills in the distance. Below to the right is the northern end of Loweswater. A few hundred metres after the end of the woods just before a line of trees, leave the path to go through a kissing gate on the right in the stone wall and into the trees **(I)**.

Bear right to descend on the track as it heads diagonally, and sometimes steeply, through Holme Wood crossing a series of forest paths. You need to take care when going down this track, particularly after rain when it can be slippery. At the bottom of the wood, the track emerges onto the main lakeside path by a gate. There is a conveniently placed bench here! **(J)**.

Go through this gate and follow the path as it bears right and then left past two National Trust properties. Proceed on the path to the National Trust car park. Go through the car park to arrive near Maggie's Bridge **(F)**.

Retrace your steps back to the end of the public footpath at the road junction. Turn right and walk 400 metres to take the road on your right signposted "Kirkstile Inn" Walk down the road to Loweswater church and the end of the walk.

Walk 7(b), Loweswater Church and Crummock Water: 2½ miles

Follow Walk 7(a) as far as **(D)**, then take the road to the left of the telephone box to walk a few hundred metres back to the church.

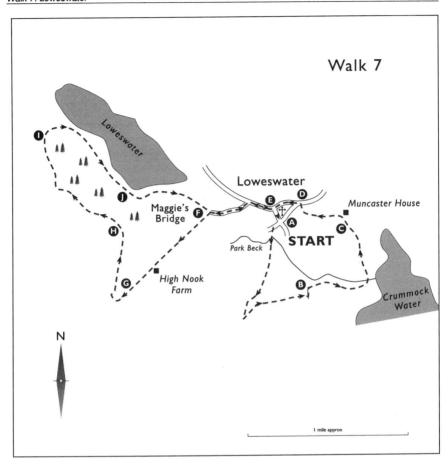

Walk 7(c), Maggie's Bridge, Holme Wood and Loweswater: 4½ miles

Leave the church **(A)** and grounds, turn right and walk up the road to the junction where there is a sign for the Kirkstile Inn, with the village hall on the corner. Now follow the directions for Walk 7(a) from **(E)**. Alternatively, after viewing the church, you can drive to the National Trust car park at Maggie's Bridge and start the walk from there.

Walk 8: Torpenhow, Ireby and Boltongate
Real Norman, redundancy and roof of stone

Location: St Michael's Church (NY205398) is at Torpenhow, 7 miles from Cockermouth and 14 miles from Carlisle on a minor road off the A591 east of Bothel.

Distance: Walk 8(a), Torpenhow, Ireby and Boltongate: 7 miles; Walk 8(b), Torpenhow and Ireby: 5½ miles.

Map: OS Outdoor Leisure 4: The English Lakes North Western area.

Terrain: These walks are mainly on the level along very quiet country lanes and farm tracks. Walk 8(b) omits the slightly busier road to Boltongate.

Churches: St Michael, Torpenhow; Ireby Old Church; St James, Ireby; All Saints, Bolton..

Car parking: Parking is available outside St Michael's Church at Torpenhow.

The Churches
St Michael, Torpenhow

If you have difficulty in finding Torpenhow it may be because you need to pronounce it as "Trepenna". This ancient name, according to the church guidebook, refers to a settlement, on a "rising topped hill", which long pre-dated the lovingly preserved and restored 12th-century church, which now stands adjacent to farm buildings at the end of this small hamlet.

You enter by a porch, which serves to protect the original Norman doorway (and its sundial!) from the elements and which contains the stone effigy of a lady. Once inside the church, the beautifully restored stonework gives a feeling of uniformity in what Simon Jenkins (*England's Thousand Best Churches*) refers to as "Cumbria's most complete Norman interior". The church is mostly built of sandstone from the nearby Solway Plain and it is thought that the Normans deliberately used its varying colours to enhance the splendour of the building. This is particularly marked in the chancel arch, which is one of the outstanding original features of the building. The arch leads, in turn, to a long chancel that draws the eye to the altar and the stained glass window behind it.

Although the church has been remodelled several times it has not been excessively Victorianised. There is, in fact, very little out of character with the early conception of the church, that is, before you look upwards in the nave! Here you find a flat wooden ceiling adorned with painted garlands of flowers and cupids. It was apparently bought from a London livery company hall at the time of its demolition and given to the church in 1689 by a Mr Thomas Addison, a relative of the famous essayist, Joseph Addison. Whatever its origins, it has been left untouched by subsequent restorers and it now provides an interesting curiosity.

Among the other features of interest are:

❖ The Norman baptismal font, with its mythical carvings, which stands on a later, possibly 15th-century shaft.

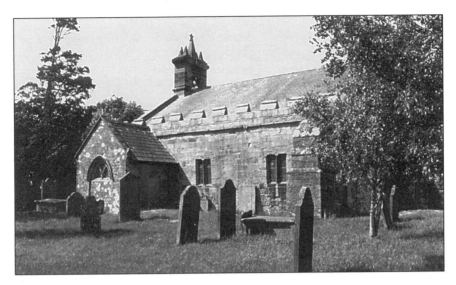

St Michael, Torpenhow

❖ The stone coffin slab inserted in the blocked west doorway.

❖ The crude carved capitals of the chancel arch. The south side shows animal and humans facing intertwined devil-like figures on the north side.

❖ The beautifully carved Jacobean pulpit and choir stalls.

❖ Some substantial stones in the walls which probably came from the nearby Roman fort of Caermote.

Information available in the church

❶ *The Parish Church of St Michael, Torpenhow: a guide and historical notes*, Wittley.

❶ *The Parish Church of St Michael, Torpenhow*, David Grech. A set of notes for reference, particularly on the stonework.

Ireby Old Church

About midway between Torpenhow and Ireby, standing in splendid isolation in a field, are the remains of another 12th-century church. It seems likely that this was built on the site of an even earlier Saxon church. This is now known as "Ireby Old Church", and it served the villagers of Ireby until 1845, when a new church dedicated to St James was built in the village itself. At that time, the nave and north aisle of the old church were demolished, the remains of the chancel were enclosed by a door and a bell turret was erected. The font and some ancient carved stones were transferred to the new church. Although the original church was subsequently maintained and used for occasional services, inevitably it had to close. In 1971, it was officially declared redundant and a year later it was taken under the wing of the Redundant Churches Fund (now The Churches Conservation Trust). This

The chancel of Ireby Old Church

simple building is only some 30 feet in length and its crude stone floor and rough wooden benches serve to engender a sense of history and remoteness.

Among the other features of interest are:

❖ The 17th-century memorial to George Crage of Prior Hall, the badly faded wording on which reads "who faithfully served Queen Elizabeth, King James, Prince Henry and Charles, King of England".

❖ The grave slabs with shears and a sword in the east wall.

❖ Two pillars, once used as gateposts in Ireby, re-erected outside the chancel where they once stood in the original nave.

Information available in the church:

❶ Hand-held information board.

❶ Leaflets about The Churches Conservation Trust (formerly the Redundant Churches Fund).

St James, Ireby

This was built in 1845-46 to replace the old church described above. It was considerably restored in 1961 and presents the appearance of a well cared for modern church. Inside, it is plain and simple with few monuments, unlike many other parish churches of the same period.

Of historical interest, transferred from the old church, are the 12th-century font at the back of the church and some stone coffin slabs in the walls of the entrance porch and in the churchyard walls opposite the porch.

There are two illustrations of interest: a pencil sketch of the old chapel before 1846; and a photograph of the Ireby Chalice, a very rare church vessel

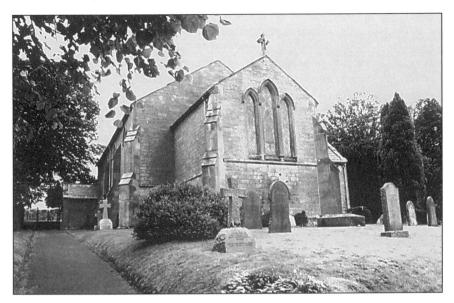

St James, Ireby

from Elizabethan times, probably from the old church, now kept in Carlisle Cathedral.

Information available in the church:

❶ *The Ireby Churches.*

❶ *Ireby Old Church Cumbria*, Redundant Churches Fund.

All Saints, Bolton

Although the church is within Boltongate, it is adjacent to Bolton Hall and in the parish of the Boltons and hence perhaps the name found on the notice-board: All Saints, Bolton. The church stands prominently, by the Bell Church Institute, formerly the schoolroom and now the church hall, at a crossroads, with fine views down to the valley below with glimpses of Skiddaw to the south-west.

The present church, dating from the 15th century, is believed to be on the site of a much earlier Norman church. Nikolaus Pevsner *(The Buildings of England: Cumberland and Westmorland)* describes the current building as "one of the architectural sensations of Cumbria" due to the surprising nature of the interior. The unusual feature here is the stone tunnel-vaulting, which you see above you in the nave and transepts. This particular type of structure, also found in some churches in Scotland, apparently came from southern France. The walls are especially thick and supported by buttresses in order to sustain the weight of the heavy roof. The oil lamps on the pews have been carefully converted to electricity to preserve the uncluttered purity of this powerful ceiling.

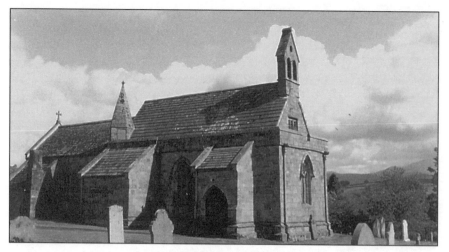

All Saints, Bolton

Among the other features of interest are:

❖ The solid old font, on the right as you enter, which is possibly Saxon.

❖ The wall tablets in the chancel commemorating a rector and two of his two sons, both of whom fell in the First World War.

❖ The small window in the south wall of the chancel, possibly once there for lepers to witness the church service.

❖ The stained glass window of St Paul on the south wall of the nave, by the noted designer Charles Kempe.

Charles Kempe (1837-1907), and the company which carried on his work until 1934, were responsible for the design and production of some 5000 stained glass windows throughout the UK and overseas. He also designed other church adornments including screens, altar panelling and church vestments. There is an information leaflet, for reference purposes, in All Saints Church which lists other churches with Kempe windows (see, for example, Walk 3, St Kentigern; Walk 11, St Michael, Walk 13, St Andrew and Walk 18, St Andrew).

Information available in the church

❶ A set of notes for reference on the stained glass windows designed by Charles Kempe.

The Walks

Walk 8(a), Torpenhow, Ireby and Boltongate: 7 miles

After visiting the church at Torpenhow, leave the churchyard by the main gate **(A)**, return to the minor road and turn left to pass the farm buildings. Follow the road out into open countryside. This is a very quiet undulating road affording views over the valley on your left of Boltongate and All Saints Church; on your right, glimpses of Binsey, the northern most fell, and ahead the Caldbeck Fells.

After about a mile the road winds down to cross the Cockshot Beck and then, some 200 metres further on, it passes a track off to the left to Prior Hall **(B)**. Ignore this, you will come back to this spot on your return journey.

The Old Church of Ireby now comes into view in a field to your right. Continue along the minor road for some 400 metres to take the metalled lane on the right. Almost immediately, there is a gate on your right. Go through the gate and follow the path across the field to Ireby Old Church **(C)**.

After visiting the church, return to the metalled lane, turn right and walk up the track for about 800 metres to pass New Park and then continue straight ahead for a further 800 metres to reach another quiet road **(D)**.

Turn left and stay on this road which will take you into Ireby. After about a hundred metres a signpost "Ireby ¼" confirms you are heading in the right

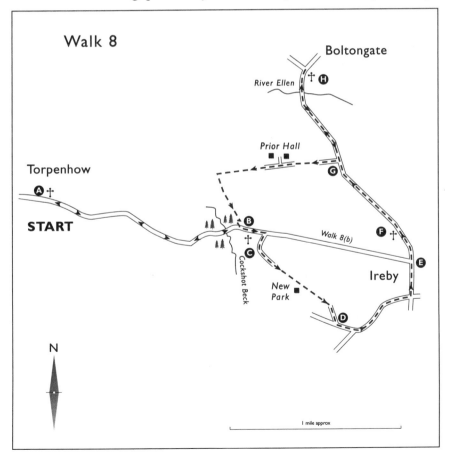

direction. The road descends into the village, passing Ireby Hall Farm and then the finely carved market cross on your right, to meet a junction. Turn left at the Lion pub, in the direction of Mealsgate, Caldbeck and Carlisle. After a short distance, at Bank Top Cottage, you pass a signpost indicating a minor road to Torpenhow **(E)**.

Continue straight ahead for a few hundred metres, passing the former Wesleyan Chapel (1870) on your left, to arrive at Ireby's "new" church of St James **(F)**.

After visiting the church, leave by the main gate at the front and turn left. Now follow this slightly busier road to pass Woodlands Hotel, a former vicarage, and after about 800 metres you pass an entrance to Prior Hall **(G)**.

Continue straight ahead and, after about another 800 metres, the road crosses the River Ellen to enter Boltongate, passing the splendid former vicarage on the right, before reaching a road junction where you will find All Saints Church, Bolton **(H)**.

After visiting the church, admire the view of Skiddaw as you retrace your steps back down the road to take the turning on your right to Prior Hall **(G)**.

Follow this farm track past Prior Hall farm buildings and keep on the same track as it bears left between Priory Cottages and Priory Mill to rejoin the minor road on which you began the walk **(B)**.

Turn right and go back along the tree-lined road for just over a mile, appreciating the views of the Solway Firth as the road descends to Torpenhow Church and the end of the walk.

Walk 8(b), Torpenhow and Ireby: 5½ miles

Follow Walk 8(a) from Torpenhow **(A)** as far Ireby's "new" church **(F)**. Then retrace your steps about 300 metres and turn right down the narrow lane **(E)**, which takes you back to Torpenhow in two miles.

Walk 9: Ainstable and Armathwaite
Bridge, Benchmark and Bascodykes

Location: St Michael and All Angels Church (NY530468) is on the northern outskirts of Ainstable village. Ainstable is located about 10 miles north of Penrith to the east of the A6.

Distance: 6 miles.

Map: OS Outdoor Leisure 5: The English Lakes North Eastern area.

Terrain: This is mostly on field paths and forest tracks with a short section on a country road. It is generally on the level but there is one gradual climb through the forest.

Churches: St Michael and All Angels, Ainstable; Christ and St Mary, Armathwaite.

Car parking: There is a car park outside Ainstable Church.

The Churches
St Michael and All Angels, Ainstable

The red sandstone Gothic-style church of St Michael and All Angels sits on a hill overlooking Ainstable. Its commanding position makes it a prominent land mark for miles around, although less so since 1983 when its 65-foot tower had to be dismantled because of faulty workmanship. Materials from the tower were used in the subsequent construction of a small but quite elaborate porch built in its place.

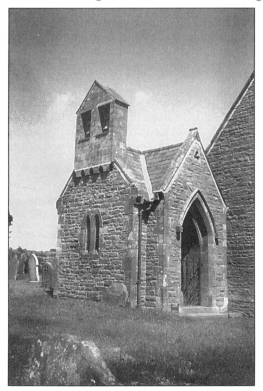

The porch of St Michael and All Angels, Ainstable

There has been a church here for at least 900 years. The present building dates from 1872 and replaced a church built around 100 years earlier. Over the centuries, there have been many patrons from within and outside the parish. During the 15th and 16th centuries, the church was connected with the local nunnery at Croglin Water which supplied its priests but this ceased following the dissolution of the nunnery in 1534. Well-known local families associated with the church have included the Dentons,

Dacres and Featherstonehaughs and, most notably, for many years from 1685, the Aglionbys.

Entry to the well-kept grounds is via the lych-gate, which was built from the wood of an old battleship after the First World War. It is Ainstable's War Memorial and was restored in 1998.

Inside is a feast of Victorian splendour: the nave with a high ceiling and exposed beams, the chancel arch with its intricately carved oak screen incorporating a metal gate, the chancel with carved choir stalls, the south transept housing an organ by Harrison and Harrison the Rolls-Royce of organ builders, stained glass windows in the west and east walls and several memorial plaques commemorating members of notable local families and others. However, despite all of this there remains a sense of spaciousness.

Among the other features of interest are:

❖ The stained glass east window by the noted Newcastle manufacturer William Wailes. It was dedicated in 1877 to Jane wife of Charles Featherstonehaugh of Stanfield Hall.

❖ The Millennium Map 2000, a framed embroidery of the parish with 55 symbols of local interest, on the north wall.

❖ A memorial tablet on the south wall of the chancel to John Yeates Bell who was killed whilst serving in the Confederate Army during the American Civil War.

❖ The altar frontal from 1995 which has appropriate pastoral designs and was produced locally.

❖ Sandstone effigies of John Aglionby and his wife Katherine Denton, one on each side of the altar; she died in 1428. Because of the close connection between the Aglionby family and Ainstable church, the effigies were transferred from St Cuthbert's Church, Carlisle following its demolition in 1778.

Information available in the church

❶ A leaflet, *The Parish Church of St Michael and All Angels: A Brief history of the Church.*

❶ On the notice board at the west end, information about the stained glass windows.

Christ and St Mary, Armathwaite

Armathwaite, meaning hermit's clearing, lies in the Eden valley. Its castle was once the seat of the Skelton family and in Richard Skelton's will the local church is referred as being "built before 1688". A kinsman, John Skelton who lived in the castle was poet laureate to Henry VIII.

The church is a small, red sandstone building, which looks as though it is almost built into the hillside, surrounded by its sloping graveyard. It dates from around 1650. Sadly, it became so dilapidated that for a while it was used as a cattle shed, before being restored to its present splendid simplicity.

It is a low, single chamber with exposed thick beams and bare walls and

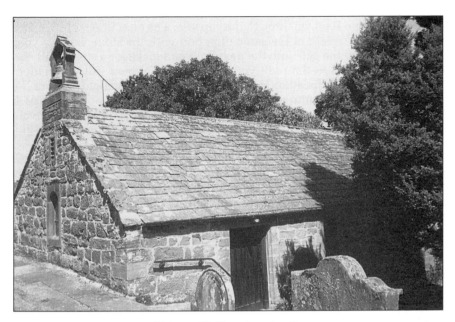

Christ and St Mary, Armathwaite

solid pews. There are circular stained glass windows on the west and south walls with dedications. The grander east window dates from 1914 and was produced from a design by Sir Edward Burne-Jones, the associate of William Morris, by Morris & Co. (see also Walk 29, Jesus Church, Troutbeck). The church banner on the altar reproduces the Christ and St Mary of the Burne-Jones window.

Armathwaite and Ainstable churches are now part of the same group of churches but, as buildings, their only common feature is the attractive red stone used in their construction. However, they do provide an extremely interesting contrast in styles for this walk.

The Walk

Go through the waymarked kissing gate in the corner of the car park, near to the west end of the church **(A)**. Below to the left you can see Ainstable Methodist Church, formerly the Wesleyan Chapel, of 1861.Turn right and walk on the public footpath up to another kissing gate with two waymarks. Go through this gate and turn left. Walk down the field boundary with the hedge on your left to a stile and gate in the corner of the field. Go over the stile and carry on in the same direction and over another stile. Carry on through a gate leading to a short green lane by the side of a house to reach a minor road **(B)**.

Cross the road and go through the gate to take the public footpath to Armathwaite. The footpath runs alongside the fields' boundaries. Ahead there are views of the Eden Valley with Armathwaite over to the left. At the end of the second field, go through the gapstile. The direction is shown by a yellow waymark. Walk in the same direction with the stone wall on your right. Go through the gate into the next field and make for a stone wall and trees ahead. Ahead to the right you can see the Drybeck railway viaduct which carries the Carlisle-Settle railway. At the end of the field, go over the stone stile to emerge onto a broad farm track with three public footpath signs. Turn left, in the direction indicated for Oatlands Cottage, and walk straight down the broad path. At the bottom go through a gate to arrive at a minor road(C).

Turn left and walk down for a few hundred metres to a public footpath sign to Armathwaite on the right immediately after a bridge over a tributary of the Eden. Take this path and after a few metres cross the waymarked stile and continue along the grassy area with the River Eden on the right. Follow the river upstream to Armathwaite Bridge. The bridge has been standing since 1701 when it replaced the ford, which had previously been the only means of crossing the river. The riverbank path leads you to a set of stone steps at the left-hand edge of the bridge. Go up the steps to come out on a pavement. You need to turn right but, before doing so, you might like to enjoy the contrasting upstream and downstream views. Having turned right, proceed over the bridge into the village. Keep on the pavement until you reach a road junction where you turn right. Walk along the road for about a hundred metres then take the narrow road to the left to walk up to Armathwaite Church gate. Go through the gate and up the steep path through the churchyard to the entrance of the church (D).

Leaving the churchyard by the gate you entered, retrace your route to Armathwaite Bridge and go down the same steps to the river level. Turn left to go under the bridge, going over a stile, across a sandy section and through a gate onto the section of the public footpath which runs partly through the grounds of Armathwaite Place. Follow the path as, initially, it runs alongside the river and then climbs up with the river below on your right. When you have ascended to about 30 metres above the river, you might spot the flat-layered rocky outcrops of Penrith sandstone in the water. At this point you reach a junction of paths and you follow the waymark to the left. In a few metres turn left again to go uphill (apparently doubling back to where you have come from). The path bends to the right and then, after a few metres, you reach a waymark post. The waymark is a little unclear as it seems to suggest going straight ahead, however, you need to turn right. Follow the woodland path until it arrives at a stile and a doggy gate in a stone wall.

Cross the stile and climb a short way up to a level section where there are a number of large rocks. On the largest of these is a sculpture with carvings of various pieces of a walker's equipment ranging from boots and socks to a rucksack. This is one of the Eden Benchmarks (E).

The Eden Benchmarks were commissioned by The East Cumbria Countryside Project to mark the new Millennium. They consist of ten carved stone sculptures which also function as seats. They are situated at various locations along the entire length of the River Eden. Each one is by a different sculptor

and has relevance for its particular site. The benchmark here is called "Vista" and is by Graeme Mitcheson of St Bees and Lazonby.

After admiring the sculpture and getting your breath back, carry on along the broad path. There are further stretches of uphill walking for the next 800 metres or so until the path comes out via a stile just beyond the Forestry Commission sign for Coombs wood. Go over the stile and turn left to walk past Coombshead Cottage and Coombshead to a telephone box (E).

Beside the telephone box, a wooden seat provides an excuse to sit for a moment or so. A plaque shows that this is "A peace offering 8th June 1946". Opposite the box is a road to Longdales. Go up this road and at the hamlet of Longdales take the lane on the left marked "To Bridleway". Walk along between fields and turn right over a stile near a gate at a public footpath sign to Bascodyke House. The meaning of this unusual name has not been firmly established but is generally understood to be a "village dyke". Walk along the field edge with the broken stone wall on your left. There are extensive views over open country on both sides. At the end of the first field bear left through a gateway and then immediately right into the next field to continue in the same direction but with the hedge now on your right. At the end of this field, go onto the wide farm track with stone walls on either side. Go through the farm gate at Bascodyke Head farm, turn left through the farmyard and bear right past the side of the farm house, ignoring the track off to the left leading to the back of the house, and after a few metres turn left through a gateway and follow the track until it reaches a metal gate. Go through the gate and proceed along the metalled road past Bascodyke and Bascodyke Foot where the road turns right. Follow the road as it climbs quite steeply for a few hundred metres to the junction with the road leading to Ainstable (**F**).

Turn left and walk the 800 metres or so to Ainstable. Ainstable Churcn can be seen sitting on its hill overlooking the village. At the crossroads go straight across and walk through the village to the signpost to the church on the left. Walk up the narrow road, past the Sunday School and Church Institute (1905) to arrive back at the church and the end of the walk.

Walk 10: Askham and Lowther
Lowther family, Lowther land, Lowther river

Location: St Peter's Church (NY518238) is just west of Askam village on a minor road leading to the Lowther Estate. Askham is 4 miles south of Penrith.

Distance: Walk 10(a), Askham and Lowther: 6 miles; Walk 10(b), Askham and Lowther, omitting Helton: 2½ miles; Walk 10(c), Askham only: 3½ miles.

Map: OS Outdoor Leisure 5: The English Lakes North Eastern area.

Terrain: Mainly on the level on public footpaths with short sections on minor roads. Walks 10(a) and 10(b) include one short steep descent.

Churches: St Peter, Askham; St Michael, Lowther.

Car parking: A limited amount of parking is available opposite St Peter's Church.

The Churches
St Peter, Askham

The church is just outside Askham village in a quiet wooded spot near the River Lowther. It was built in 1832 by Robert Smirke, architect of Lowther Castle, on the site of a much older church and incorporates, as the south transept, the former burial chapel of the Sandford family from nearby Askham Hall. The Hall was bought by the Lowther family around 300 years ago and is now the home of the Earl of Lonsdale. Of neo-Norman design, the church has a north-west tower and a single-level roof. The date 1832 appears above and on the west door. Nikolaus Pevsner *(The Buildings of England:*

St Peter, Askham

Cumberland and Westmorland) found it architecturally depressing, but it does not seem so and, in any event, today's visitor probably discounts this in favour of its peaceful setting in its well-kept graveyard and the welcoming notice board.

In addition to its dedication to St Peter, the church has also been dedicated to St Kentigern, the Celtic saint (see Walk 3, St Kentigern, Crossthwaite).

Inside, the nave and chancel are one and there is an arcaded north aisle. All the windows (which are all round-headed except for one) are of clear leaded glass providing plenty of light to the interior. The church is plain and uncluttered giving a restful atmosphere; this applies particularly to the south transept used as a baptistry with its simple small font, from 1661, in a large open space.

Among the other features of interest are:

❖ The west gallery with four rows of pews.

❖ The old parish chest with three locks in the north aisle.

❖ The memorial tablets to the Sandford family in the south transept.

❖ On the north arcade, looking towards the Sandford Chapel, a solitary carved sandstone head.

❖ The quilted altar frontal, made by Josephine Ratcliff of Penrith, a welcome addition to the church furnishings for the new millennium. One frontal, from the set of four available, is used at the appropriate liturgical season in the Church's year. The designer has incorporated references to both St Peter and St Kentigern in the set.

Information available in the church:

❶ A leaflet, *Altar Frontals at Askham Church, Cumbria*, Josephine Ratcliff.

❶ A notice on the east wall of the south transept giving information about the Sandford Chapel.

St Michael, Lowther

The church stands in an isolated but magnificent setting in the parkland of the Lowther Estate and in sight of the splendid ruins of Lowther Castle. Its lonely position arises because the original village, lying just to the south of the church gates, was pulled down and rebuilt as Lowther Newtown in the 1680s. This was part of a scheme by John, 1st Viscount Lonsdale to rebuild Lowther Hall, the predecessor of Lowther Castle, and the church.

Between the entrance to the churchyard and the church itself is the Lowther Mausoleum in which can be seen the seated figure of the Earl Lonsdale. Nearby are plots where other members of the family are buried. Viewed from the gateway, the church's structure looks a little unbalanced partly due to the mixture of styles in several reconstructions and extensions carried out over centuries. In essence, a Norman church was enlarged in the 13th century, reconstructed in the 17th and acquired a 19th-century vestry and porch.

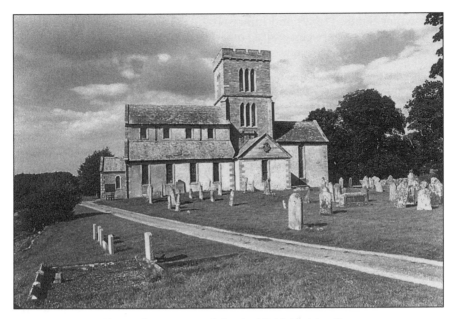

The much reconstructed church of St Michael, Lowther

The 1st Viscount's work in the 1680s involved taking down the outer walls and rebuilding them around the existing pillars and arches.

Inside, none of this matters because here is a wealth of interest, both as to architecture and furnishings. Entry is through the 19th-century porch, where ancient grave slabs are displayed, and under the 18th-century gallery to the nave. On the north side is a beautiful Norman arcade of pillars leading to the north aisle and a similar arcade, of about 1250, on the south side. The tower crossing leads to the chancel through elegant Gothic arches. Much of the space in the transepts and elsewhere is given over to ornate and sometimes magnificent Lowther memorials.

To some this is a place of surprises and delights. Others might find the predominance of Lowther memorials a distraction from the building's main purpose.

Among the other features of interest are:

❖ In the porch, a Norse tombstone showing the two Viking ships with warriors, possible evidence of the Norse presence before the building of the Norman church.

❖ In the north transept a number of Lowther memorials including the free standing marble tomb chest of William, Earl of Lonsdale who died in 1844.

❖ In the south transept, three Lowther memorials including one of Sir John

Lowther Senior (1637) and Junior (1675), consisting of two white busts with a skull in between resting on an ornate, garlanded tablet.

❖ The 18th-century pulpit.

❖ The east window. This has references to the 5th Earl "a great English sportsman" and his wife, the Countess of Lonsdale "a pioneer of home nursing in Cumberland". The right light shows St Cuthbert. The left light shows St George and the dragon to fulfil Hugh Cecil's wish to commemorate the victory of the Allies in World War 2 and "record the part played by the men and women of the parish of the Lowther estate".

The Lowther family have lived at Lowther for over 800 years. The family title "Lonsdale" derives from the River Lune, one of the four historical divisions of Westmorland. Apart from being important landowners, the family is also known for its entrepreneurial activities and sporting links. Lonsdale belts were named after the 5th Earl for his efforts in gaining respectability for boxing and the Lowther Horse Trials are held annually in August.

The Walks

Walk 10(a), Askham and Lowther: 6 miles

Leave Askham Church **(A)** by the west door. Turn left and walk up the church pathway to go through a gateway. Carry on with woods on your left and the new cemetery on your right and go through the gate leading into a field. Turn left with the fence on your left and proceed along the field boundary, passing a "private" gate near a waymark showing your direction. Walk in the direction indicated, with the fence and wood on your left, go through a gate and carry on until you reach a public footpath sign. At this point looking behind you can see Askham Hall. Turn right and keep on the path to go over a stile onto a broad farm track with a stone wall and then a fence on your right and a fence on the left. Continue and, where the track bears to the left, cross a stile to the right of a gate, into a wooded area, a few yards before a Lowther Estate "no access" sign. Follow the track for a short distance to exit from the woods via a stone stile near a gate onto a narrow road **(B)**.

Turn left and walk down this pleasant country lane for about 800 metres. There are trees on the left and the small village of Helton can be seen over to the right. Just before Crookwath Bridge, look out for a public footpath sign on the right. The River Lowther is now visible ahead **(C)**.

Cross the stile and walk to the left to cross another stile. Head towards the river via a little footbridge, then walk straight ahead with the river on your left. This is an attractive riverside walk and takes you via a ladder stile, a stone stile, footbridge, and two more ladder stiles to a gap in a broken stone wall. The path goes a little away from the river at this point. Bear slightly right to a waymark post to the left of a metal gate, then head for another waymark post and then a waymarked stile, which is half hidden over the fence on your right. Cross the stile and turn left with the fence on your left and walk in the same direction passing a waymarked stile standing in splen-

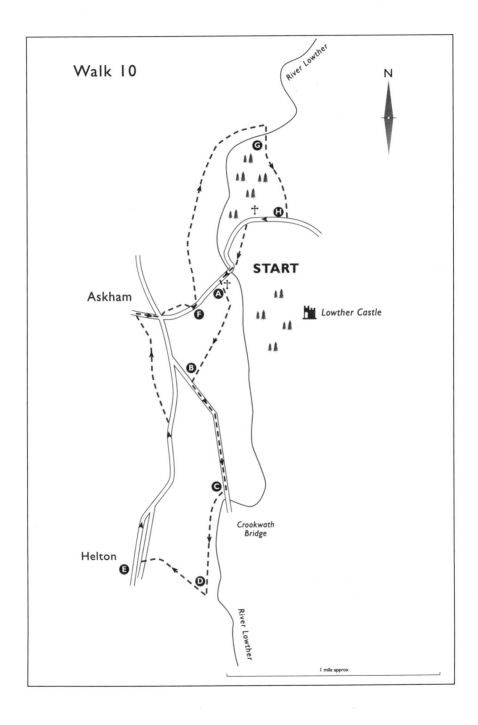

Walk 10

River Lowther

N

Askham

START

Lowther Castle

Crookwath
Bridge

Helton

River Lowther

1 mile approx

did isolation and a waymarked post. Bear left over the field to a small foot-bridge over a little stream **(D)**.

Go across the footbridge, turn right and walk with the wire fence and a broken wall on your right until you come to a waymarked gate. Go through the gate and walk up the lonnen between stone walls. After a fairly steep climb, the village of Helton appears ahead. Continue on the lonnen to emerge via a stile next to a gate onto a path leading to a road. Cross the road and continue on the public bridleway between houses to reach another road **(E)**.

You are now in Helton and need to turn right to proceed through the village. There is a steep village green on the left and the Helton Inn on your right. The road passes some interesting old and new buildings including the former Wesleyan Chapel (1867), before arriving at a road junction where you turn left. Walk along this busier road for about 600 metres. Just before a copse on your right look for a stone stile on your left; it is somewhat concealed and there is no footpath sign. Cross the stile into the field and bear slightly right to reach a wall and keeping this wall on your right walk through the fields going over two stiles. After the second stile walk to the ladder stile, ahead across the field beyond the telegraph post, and go over this stile to arrive in Askham. Walk between the houses to reach a road and turn right to go through the village, crossing a main road to go down a lane between The Queen's Head on the left and Askham Stores on the right. Continue along this lane, passing the Old Post Office on your left and The Old School on your right, to reach the banked village green on your right. The lane bears right to join a minor road **(F)**.

Turn left and proceed in the same direction the short distance to the last group of cottages at the end of the green on your left, just before the Punch Bowl Inn on the right. Just to the left of these cottages, there is a gateway with a public bridleway sign. Go through the gateway and follow the bridleway as it bears left between barns then through a waymarked gate onto a broad lonnen. You might like to stop to admire Askham Hall on your right. Proceed the short distance to take the public footpath on the right, going over a stile to head diagonally left across the field to a ladder stile in the far corner. Go over the stile into the woods and proceed down for 100 metres or so to arrive at a junction with a broad forest path. Turn left to go in the direction indicated by a waymark. Follow the clear path which is fairly level at first but then zig-zags up and down through the wood and finally descends quite steeply to a metal gate which leads to a metalled road a few metres further on. Turn right, go over the stile and cross the hump backed bridge. There is also a bridge for estate vehicles to the left **(G)**.

You are now enjoying more of the grounds of the Lowther Estate. Walk straight ahead on the metalled road, via a metal gate, and soon the remains of Lowther Castle come into view. This magnificent Gothic shell is all that remains of the former castellated mansion built by the 1st Earl between 1806 and 1811. The Lowther family lived there until its closure in 1936. Over to the right you can see Lowther Church between its surrounding trees. Keep straight ahead, ignoring a path coming in from the left, and continue past a waymarked cattle grid until you reach a junction. Turn right and walk along the straight road to a gate and a cattle grid. Cross the cattle grid and walk to the right to the gate leading into the church grounds and Lowther Church **(H)**.

Leave the church grounds by the gate you entered and cross the road to a public footpath sign. Go through the gate into the field and bear to the right to head for a waymarked stile, which is about 100 metres from the right-hand corner of the field. You might pause here to enjoy an excellent view of the castle. Go over the stile and walk through the woods. In a short while you will catch glimpses of Askham Church through the trees over to the right. Carry on to a green metal seat near a junction of paths. Turn right onto the white waymarked permitted footpath as it descends quite steeply to reach a bend in a road. Take care as you turn left to walk over the bridge to arrive back at Askham Church and the end of the walk.

Walk 10(b), Askham and Lowther, omitting Helton: 2½ miles

Leave the church grounds by the gate onto the road and turn left to walk up to Askham. As you reach the village, there is a banked green area on your right overlooked by houses. At the end of the first group of cottages on your right, there is a gateway with a public bridleway sign. This is the gateway described after point **(F)** in Walk 10(a). Now follow the directions for Walk 10(a) from the gateway.

Walk 10(c), Askham only: 3½ miles

Follow Walk 10(a) as far as Askham village green **(F)**. Turn left and walk straight ahead on the road out of the village for 400 metres to return to the church and the end of the walk.

Walk 11: Barton, Pooley Bridge and Dacre
Farms, fish and friendly bears

Location: St Michael's Church, Barton (NY487264) is just off the B5320 about 3 miles west of Penrith.

Distance: Walk 11(a), Barton, Pooley Bridge and Dacre: 11 miles; Walk 11(b), Barton and Pooley Bridge: 6 miles; Walk 11(c), Pooley Bridge and Dacre: 5 miles.

Map: OS Outdoor Leisure 5: The English Lakes North Eastern area.

Terrain: This is almost entirely on public footpaths and bridleways. It is generally on the level, although there is some steady but gentle climbing in the early stages of Walks 11(a) and 11(b).

Churches: St Michael, Barton; St Paul, Pooley Bridge; St Andrew, Dacre.

Car parking: There is limited parking outside Barton Church. For those starting from Pooley Bridge there is limited parking next to St Paul's Church as well as pay and display car parks on either side of the bridge.

The Churches
St Michael, Barton

At first sight this church appears to stand in the middle of nowhere. There is not a village as such here and apparently there never has been one. However, closer inspection reveals that there are farm buildings and dwellings, including the old vicarage, behind the church. It is not surprising, therefore, that there are several old footpaths in the vicinity, which once must have drawn the congregation from a wide area.

St Michael, Barton with its central tower

The church, which dates from 1150, is still substantially Norman in appearance although it has been extended and altered over time. It has obviously been carefully restored and lovingly maintained. The central tower catches the eye. Inside you find a real gem and a lovely surprise. The centre of the nave is occupied by a double rounded arch, which forms the base for the tower. The space between allows access and a view to the chancel behind. This structure once served as a barrier to the ordinary worshipper who would be kept at a discreet distance from the priest and dignitaries beyond. Nowadays, an altar stands under the arch thus allowing a much more intimate form of worship. No one should now feel excluded here, although visitors are gently reminded to remove any muddy boots! There is certainly a lot to see and visitors are even invited to put the lights on to have a better look.

Among the various memorials in the church, perhaps the Wordsworth connection is one worth noting in particular. A small brass plaque on the north wall of the chancel indicates that Richard Wordsworth, the grandfather of the poet, who died in 1760, is buried there. On the opposite wall there is also a memorial to Ann Myers, William Wordsworth's aunt. She was married to a minister at Barton, the Revd Thomas Myers.

An archway from the chancel on the south side leads through to the Lancaster Chapel, where there are three further memorial tablets to members of the family: John, the poet's cousin, and his first and second wives, Anne and Elisabeth. The chapel was restored in 1956, under Canon Ernest Hudson, as indicated on a wall tablet. It is now regarded as a "Chapel of Peace".

Among the other features of interest are:

❖ The window in the north wall to a former parishioner who married in Canada and lived to a fine old age.

❖ The face carved on the base of the arch to the left of the pulpit said to be that of Edward I or II and believed to date from about 1280.

❖ The coat of arms of George III, dated 1730, above the chancel arch. As in many other churches, this would serve as a reminder to the parishioners of the day as to where their loyalty should lie.

❖ The east window, the intricately carved lectern and the impressive choir stalls and screen in the chancel, in memory of William Hugh Parkin whose family is also remembered at Martindale (see Walk 14, St Peter).

❖ The west window showing St Michael, the Annunciation and angels by Kempe (see Walk 8, All Saints).

Information available in the church:

❶ *A Guide to St Michael's Church, Barton*, John Towler.

St Paul, Pooley Bridge

St Paul's provides a quiet and peaceful place of retreat on the busy main road through this very popular tourist spot. It is very much a modern church in relation to its two illustrious neighbours. Its foundation stone was laid in

St Paul, Pooley Bridge – a peaceful place of retreat

1867 and, as a chapel-of-ease, it depended on Barton until it became a separate parish in 1905. The Revd W. Airey, who generously donated the site to the church, is remembered in the west windows and in a plaque below, but otherwise the church, with its plain walls and windows, is devoid of Victorian dedications.

Perhaps St Paul's did not enjoy the patronage of wealthy landowners and remained instead a simpler place of worship for those who frequented the modest markets held in the village. It is interesting to note that the adjacent village hall, dated 1911, is entitled the Parkin Memorial Hall, recalling the local significance of the Parkins, patrons of Barton Church.

Nowadays St Paul's is pleased to welcome and serve the many tourists who stay in and around Pooley Bridge. A nice feature is the occasional seating found at the end of the pine pews still in use on special occasions.

Among the other features of interest are:

❖ The carved reredos behind the altar.

❖ The lancet east windows with their geometrical patterns.

❖ The embroidered kneelers.

❖ The photograph in the entrance porch, indicating the strong links which exist with a parish in Liverpool.

Information available in the church:

❶ A leaflet, *Visitors, welcome to Saint Paul's, Pooley Bridge.*

St Andrew, Dacre, close to the castle

St Andrew, Dacre

The church is nicely positioned, just off a quiet lane, in the centre of the pleasant and ancient village of Dacre. It rests within sight of the 14th-century Dacre Castle, some two miles from Dalemain House, both of which properties belong to its most important patrons, the Hasell family.

The church was Norman in period and style but was substantially rebuilt in 1810. Today the well-restored stonework, the nave with its high ceiling, the arcades creating separate aisles and the chancel with its attractive timber beams combine to make a homely, well-ordered church. However, this is probably the only church in England where visitors are greeted by bears!

The Dacre stone bears stand at the four corners of the churchyard and these unusual carved figures have given rise to a lot of speculation about their origin and meaning. It is believed that they came from the castle and the popular explanation, that they depict an encounter between a bear and a small animal, is told in the leaflet available in the church.

Although the thirty or more wall plaques can be a trifle overwhelming, they reveal some fascinating stories about the principal local families, especially the Hasells.

Among the other features of interest are:

❖ The bible of 1617 in the cabinet in the north-east corner of the nave.

❖ The two brass tablets in front of the altar each of which tells its own story.

❖ The two 9th- and 10th-century stone cross shafts by the south wall of the chancel. Their complex and intricate motifs are detailed in the guidebook available in the church.

❖ Two 20th-century windows in the south wall of the chancel: the stained glass window commemorates the untimely death in 1944 of William Somerville Marshall, a Hasell son-in-law. It is one of the earliest works of Leonard Evetts the famous 20th-century designer (see the companion volume: *Northumbria Church Walks*, Sigma Press). The other window, with scenes of Dalemain finely etched in the glass, is dedicated to Sylvia Mary McCosh, presumably William's widow who must have remarried.

❖ The lock on the south doorway (concealed by a curtain) dated 1671, bearing the initials A.P., of Lady Anne Clifford of Pembroke (see Walk 12, St Wilfred).

Information available in the church:

❸ *A short history of Dacre Parish Church and the early history of the church site*, Philippa J.F. Smith and Rachael M. Newman.

❸ *The Great Dacre Bears*, Revd Canon Peter J. Wilson.

The Walks
Walk 11(a), Barton, Pooley Bridge and Dacre: 11 miles

After visiting St Michael's Church, Barton **(A)** leave through the lych-gate and follow the minor road back to the main road. Turn right and cross the road with care to leave the road over a waymarked stone stile by a gate signposted "Public Footpath Celleron". Walk ahead up the side of the field and through a waymarked kissing gate next to a metal gate to join a track. Keep straight ahead and in a short distance pass through a small bolted wooden gate into a further field. Cross the dyke and continue round the edge of the field, with a hedge on your left, to cross a waymarked stile in the top corner. Walk straight ahead, skirting the small crag on your left, to climb to a waymarked stile ahead. Go over the stile and, bearing very slightly left, walk up the field, aiming for the waymarked corner of the fence ahead. Proceed towards the farmhouse ahead keeping the field boundary on your right. Exit, via a stile next to a gate, onto the minor road by Celleron House **(B)**.

Turn right and walk about 50 metres to a T-junction. Bear left and cross the road to go through a wooden gate marked "Footpath". Now proceed up the right-hand side of the field to take the ladder stile at the top of the field onto a track. Turn right, walk up the track to pass a cottage and continue along the track to Winder Hall Farm **(C)**.

Follow the track as it bears right in front of the farmhouse to a kissing gate. Once through the kissing gate the track becomes rough and stony. This may be a good moment to stop and admire the view behind you of Penrith and the Pennines. Go along the main track as it bears left and proceed keeping the wall and the line of trees on your left. When you reach the corner of the wall keep straight ahead to climb for a further 100 metres or so on to meet a clear path between two small cairns. Turn right along a track, which soon

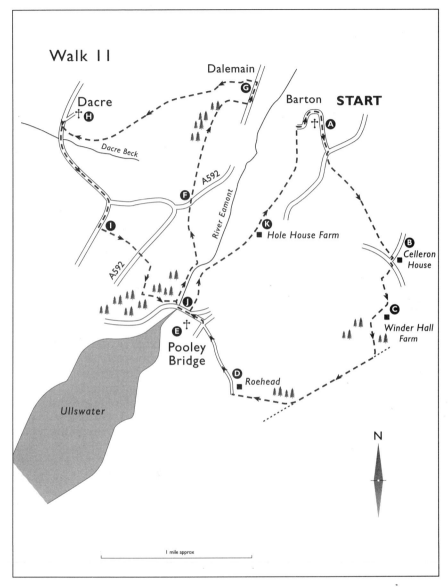

becomes more well-worn. Soon you will be rewarded with views of Ullswater ahead and Pooley Bridge to your right. Continue on this track for a few hundred metres until you just about come level with the village of Pooley Bridge below. At a small cairn, fork right off the main track and follow the broad grassy track down a short way, towards a line of trees rising from the valley. When you are level with the line of trees and the wall beside them, fork right again to descend towards the valley, keeping the trees and the wall on your right. Continue straight ahead down the grassy bank, ignoring a path off to the left, until you can see a track and a road below to the left and a wood appears on your right. Now follow the path as it bears left to descend to the track. Turn right down the track to go through a gate at Roehead and onto a metalled lane **(D)**.

Continue down Roe Head Lane stopping to enjoy the views from one of the conveniently placed benches. Shortly after passing Hillcroft Park campsite on your right, you will reach the crossroads at the entrance to Pooley Bridge. Carry straight on into the village past some pleasant cottages until you reach St Paul's Church **(E)**.

After visiting St Paul's Church, continue ahead, passing the Sun Inn on your right-hand side and then the Fish Cross.

The Fish Cross is Pooley Bridge's millennium monument bearing the two key family names of the area, Dacre, your next destination, and Hasell, of Dalemain which you will pass en route. It has a salmon on the top, a reminder that this was once the scene of an important fish market.

Continue ahead over the old bridge, which gives the name to the village, turn right and follow the public footpath sign "A592 ¾ mile" to cross the Dunmallard pay and display car park and enter a wood. Walk along the track, with the River Eamont, which flows out of Ullswater, on your right, to leave the wood through a gate. Continue straight ahead, keeping the river on your right, following the waymarks and going through several kissing gates. After a kissing gate slightly concealed behind trees, the path turns away from the river to pass a pond over to the right. After a stile next to a gate turn right and walk along the edge of the field with a wire fence on your right. This is a potentially muddy area although some small plank bridges are of assistance. Soon you exit onto the A592 via a kissing gate. Cross the busy road with care, turn left and proceed for just over 200 metres to the junction with the road to Dacre **(F)**.

(If you wish to shorten the route by about one and a half miles and omit Dalemain, then you can proceed up the road directly to Dacre in about one mile).

To continue, take the stone stile on the right and walk in the direction of the public footpath sign across the field to take a further stile. Continue ahead for about 30 metres and then bear right on the faint green track keeping close to the wire fence on your left to climb eventually to cross a stile next to a gate. This is a good place to stop to catch your breath and to admire the views of the north Pennines ahead. Walk straight ahead along the side of the fields with the wire fence on your left and go over a stile next to a gate to join a track coming from your left. With a plantation now on your left, cross another stile next to a gate as Dalemain comes fully into view. Follow the faint path towards the imposing house ahead and make for the old Dacre Bridge. However, as there is no right of way over the bridge you need to follow the waymark to a stile on your right and exit onto the A592. Turn left to cross the "new" bridge over the Dacre Beck and proceed with care for about 300 metres before turning left and going through a metal kissing gate next to a cattle grid onto the driveway of Dalemain **(G)**.

Dalemain has been in the hands of the Hasell family ever since the end of the 17th century when it was acquired by Sir Edward Hasell, a steward of Lady Anne Clifford. The original house is believed to have been built as early as the 15th century. Nowadays the house, with its splendid Georgian east front, museums, café, gift shop and gardens is open to paying visitors (except on Fridays and Saturdays when it is often used for private functions) but happily there still remains a public right of way through this part of the estate. Visitors are asked to respect the privacy of the occupants.

Follow the public footpath carefully down the drive bearing right round the back of the house, passing the car park and going through the archway into the courtyard. Turn right up the lane with the high estate wall on your left. After the broad track leaves the wall, you can view the Dacre Beck on your left. Soon you find you are following a fine line of trees on your right as you proceed for a mile or so on the carriageway that has taken generations of the Hasell family to Dacre church. The way is straight and clear and you pass through a couple of gates. The track eventually bears right and ascends slightly before passing some farm buildings. To the right is the church and ahead is Dacre Castle.

Dacre Castle is now a very pleasant private residence which has evolved out of a 14th-century pele tower, turned castle, built by William de Dacre. By the end of the 17th century, the castle was in ruins and the following century it passed into the hands of the present owners, the Hasells of Dalemain.

Continue past the castle and exit onto the road. Turn right and after some 25 metres bear right at a junction. Proceed up the lane for about 75 metres to find St Andrew's Church down a short driveway on your right **(H)**.

After visiting St Andrew's Church retrace your steps to the road and follow it down to the left, passing the sign to Penrith, to carry on in the same direction crossing the Dacre Beck. Climb steadily to pass the old vicarage on your left and, after about 800 metres, turn right at the sign for Soulby along an even quieter road. Follow the road past the telephone box and the farm and, about 150 metres further on, take the public bridleway for the A592 and Pooley Bridge, via a stile on the left **(I)**.

Continue straight ahead down the side of the field keeping the wire fence on your right. Go through a gate and proceed ahead for a short distance before bearing right to exit onto the A592 via a kissing gate. Cross over with due care and continue via the stile on the public bridleway to Pooley Bridge. After a few hundred metres, at the end of a short section of stone wall, leave the path to cross a waymarked stile on the right. Now follow the footpath diagonally left towards the plantation surrounding Dunmallard Hill. Cross a waymarked double stile and continue in the same direction to enter the plantation by a kissing gate. Turn left and descend through the wood on the broad track to exit by the car park via a kissing gate. Now cross the bridge and proceed about 300 metres or so to the Sun Inn **(J)**.

Turn left down the right-hand side of the inn and go through the waymarked kissing gate onto a clear track. Follow the track as it bears right and passes a sewage works on your left. Proceed straight ahead with the river on your left. Eventually the path climbs away from the river, passing two waymark posts and making towards the farm buildings and a caravan site. Bear left through the waymarked gate and continue ahead between the cottages and buildings at Hole House Farm making use of the waymarks**(K)**.

At the end of the farm buildings, go over a waymarked stile next to a metal gate. Now proceed straight ahead over a series of waymarked stiles next to gates. Look out for a signpost on the right next to a waymarked kissing gate. Here you go through the gate and take the public footpath on the left signposted to Barton. Follow the narrow path between the hedgerows to a waymarked gate and into a more open area and a broader path. Continue ahead and go through the next waymarked gate. Although the path is not so obvious, keep straight ahead, following the line of the wire fence on your right. Cross the waymarked stile next to a gate and walk straight ahead, looking for finger posts at the end of the field where you join a track. Turn left down the track to pass through a waymarked gate and immediately another gate. After a further 40 metres, turn right as signposted to Barton. In a few metres, there is a sign for Barton Church on a tree on your left. Continue straight ahead along the clear broad track over the waymarked stiles next to gates to Barton Church Farm. Follow the helpful waymarks through the farm and the archway. Go past the cottages, bear left past Glebe Farm and follow the track past the old vicarage, almost hidden behind the hedge, shortly to arrive back at St Michael's Church and the end of the walk.

Walk 11(b), Barton and Pooley Bridge: 6 miles

Follow Walk 11(a) as far as The Sun Inn at Pooley Bridge and continue as from **(J)** above.

Walk 11(c), Pooley Bridge and Dacre: 5 miles

Start at St Peter's Church, Pooley Bridge **(E)** and follow Walk 11(a) to Dacre and back to Pooley Bridge.

Walk 12: Clifton and Brougham
Fields, fortresses and freeways

Location: St Cuthbert's Church (NY533271) is at the northern end of Clifton, which is on the A6 two miles south of Penrith.

Distance: Walk 12(a), Clifton and Brougham: 7 miles; Walk 12(b), Clifton and Brougham omitting Brougham Castle: 5 miles.

Map: OS Outdoor Leisure 5: The English Lakes North Eastern area.

Terrain: Walks 12(a) and 12(b) are mostly on the level along field and riverside paths and quiet country roads with two short sections on a busy road.

Churches: St Cuthbert, Clifton; St Wilfred, Brougham.

Car parking: There is limited parking outside Clifton Church.

The Churches
St Cuthbert, Clifton

The church is situated at the northern end of Clifton village. Beyond the church, looking north towards Penrith, the ground falls away steeply. Presumably, the builders of the nearby 15th-century Clifton Hall made use of this advantageous position. All that remains of the Hall, formerly a home of the Engaynes and the Wyberghs, is the restored pele tower which is a few hundred metres away over the road and which provides a useful landmark later in the walk.

The church dates from the 12th century and what is seen now is a small red

Nave and chancel of St Cuthbert, Clifton

sandstone building in a well-kept graveyard with a Norman nave and a slightly lower chancel. A restoration in 1846 included rebuilding and lengthening the chancel using the original material. There is a very short north aisle and a substantial porch.

Inside, near the entrance, are the font and a piscina. Looking towards the altar, at the east end there is an impression of length, with the long chancel divided from the nave by the 1846 screen of two columns and three arches. The windows in the west, north and south walls are of plain glass. Wood from the pre-1846 building was used in the construction of the carved pulpit and there are attractive carved choir stalls, bearing the date 1683, in the extended chancel.

There are a limited number of memorial plaques but, overall, there is no feeling of overcrowding which is sometimes associated with 19th-century restorations. Rather, a sense of spirituality prevails in this place.

Among the other features of interest are:

❖ The three lancet east window containing small 15th-century stained glass motifs of the Virgin Mary and St John.

❖ In the north aisle, the coat of arms and tablet which explains how the Wyberghs acquired the manor of Clifton.

❖ In the churchyard, near the gate a small stone marking the burial place of the Duke of Cumberland's fourteen soldiers killed in the Battle of Clifton in 1745 (see below). This was erected in 1968 by the Queen's Own Hussars.

St Wilfred, Brougham

A chapel-of-ease for the villagers living near Brougham Hall was built some time before 1393. The chapel was pulled down and rebuilt by Lady Anne Clifford (see below) in 1659.

Most of what you now see from the outside is Lady Anne's work. An attractive, single chamber, low building with a little bellcote and small arched windows; sitting peaceably in its well-kept grounds.

Once inside, it is a different story. You are presented with an eclectic mix of ornate ecclesiastical furnishings, with dark rich oak carvings predominating, yet with an overall sense of sanctity. Many of the items were introduced during the 1840s by William, a brother of the first Lord Brougham (see below), who lived at Brougham Hall and who later succeeded to the title. William also built the rose window in the east wall and Normanized the internal window arches.

The overall effect of the collection is not to everyone's taste. Nikolaus Pevsner *(The Buildings of England: Cumberland and Westmorland)* took the view that the chapel "suffered at the hands of Lord Brougham and Vaux in the 1840s". On the other hand, Sir John Betjeman *(Guide to English Parish Churches)* wrote of its "rich cathedral opulence". Simon Jenkins *(England's Thousand Best Churches)* thinks that "the chapel is a remarkable treasure house to find in the wilds of Cumbria".

Among the other features of interest are:

❖ The 14th-century glass in the two east windows.

❖ The 15th-century French carved stalls.

❖ The screen with pillars which is 15th-century English work set in 19th-century fittings.

❖ The 16th-century pulpit with interesting carvings.

Information available in the church:

❶ *Brougham Chapel, The History of the Parish of Brougham, Westmorland-in-Cumbria*, Revd T.W.H. Rutherford.

> *Lady Anne Clifford (1590-1676) was the last of the ancient and wealthy Clifford family – the only daughter of George 13th Lord Clifford and 3rd Earl of Cumberland. Widowed twice, she moved north in 1649 and spent the next 27 years managing and moving between her estates including castles at Appleby, Brougham, Brough and Skipton. She was heavily involved in restoration work in the castles and chapels in her care. She rebuilt the ancient chapel of St Ninian's at Ninekirks about two miles east of Brougham. The dedication to St Ninian reflects the traditional belief that St Ninian founded a church around here in the 5th century. Lady Anne was an indomitable lady who carried on her improvements despite Cromwellian disapproval of the military possibilities opened up by some of the restorations. Told to stop, she replied with the 17th-century equivalent of "Over my dead body!" She died at her favourite castle, Brougham, in 1676.*

St Wilfred, Brougham

The Walks

Walk 12(a), Clifton and Brougham: 7 miles

Leave the church **(A)** and grounds by the gate leading to the A6. Turn left along the pavement and continue over the railway and through the village until you reach a public bridleway sign "Clifton Dykes" on the left. (The paint on some of the sign's embossed letters is missing). Take the bridleway which soon crosses the railway. Initially, you are on a lonnen running between walls and then hedges. Continue on the bridleway and turn right at a waymark, then carry on until you come to a waymarked gate. The Battle of Clifton Moor (see below) was fought in the fields around here – although the site of the battlefield is not identified on the ground. The waymark indicates left but you need to keep to the same direction you have been walking and head across the field to a waymarked gate near another waymark also pointing the way. Now turn left, walk up the field with a wire fence on your right, and then descend to a waymarked gate **(B)**.

> *The Battle of Clifton Moor was the last battle fought on English soil and took place during the Jacobite Rebellion of 1745. In a short engagement, the rearguard of Prince Charles Edward Stuart's army drove a detachment of the Duke of Cumberland's forces from its position on Clifton Moor. The rearguard rejoined the main body as it set out for Scotland on 20 December, the Prince's 25th birthday. And so, via fighting at Falkirk and Nairn, the dwindling force made its way finally and fatefully to Culloden Moor.*

Go through the gate and walk straight ahead going through two more waymarked gates. After the second of these, a little stream runs across the path. Proceed straight ahead and in a short while a broader stream runs alongside over to your right. Carry straight on and go through a metal gate. Then bear right, negotiate the steam, and go up the grassy lonnen to a waymarked gate. After going through the gate, walk straight ahead with the hedge on your right to arrive at a metal gate. There are two power lines overhead a short distance in front of you. Carry on in the same direction, through a waymarked gate with the hedge now on your left and then through a metal gate. Continue ahead down the lonnen, pass the pylon and exit from the field via a gate onto a minor road **(C)**.

Turn left and proceed down the road, enjoying the views of the North Pennines ahead. After 800 metres you come to a road junction where you turn left onto the busier road in the direction signposted for Penrith. Walk past Tarn Hill Farm and the buildings of Low Dykes on your left. About 150 metres past Apple Dene bungalow turn right onto the metalled road, which is the entrance to High Ground Farm. (There is a public footpath sign for "Moor" on the opposite side of the road you have been walking on). Walk a couple of hundred metres, going under a power line, and just before the farm buildings go through the first (of two) metal gates on your left. Walk straight ahead with the hedge on your right and go over the stile into the next field to carry on in the same direction with the hedge now on your left. You can see Penrith ahead to the right. Go through the metal gate into the next field and

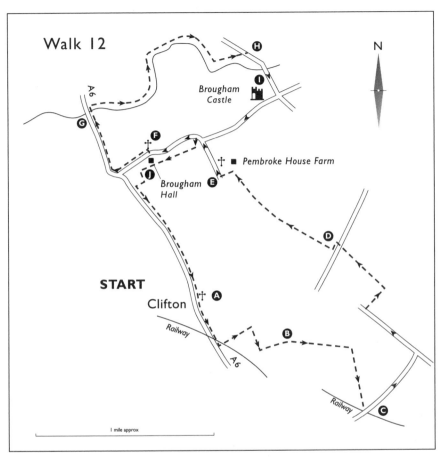

Walk 12

Brougham
Castle

Pembroke House Farm

Brougham
Hall

START

Clifton

Railway

1 mile approx

keep straight ahead to exit via a stile next to a gate onto a minor road. Turn left and walk 20 metres to come to a public footpath sign "Brougham" on your right **(D)**.

Take the footpath, which is somewhat overgrown. It runs between field edges, with trees on both sides, in a fairly straight line for about 1000 metres before exiting, via a sturdy metal gate, into a field. You can see Pembroke House Farm ahead. Walk towards the farm along the clear track with the hedge on your right. Just before the farm gate, turn left and walk down the side of the field with a stone wall on your right to cross a stone stile next to a gate and exit onto a road. Bearing right, walk a few metres past the farmhouse to a gate on your right. Near the gate is a notice with details of the "Church in the Barn" which is just through the gate **(E)**.

The Church in the Barn at Pembroke House Farm is an independent church, with a Pentecostal philosophy, which holds its services in a converted barn. After viewing the Church in the Barn, carry on in the same direction as before to walk a couple of hundred metres to a junction. Turn left and follow the road as it bears left and goes uphill past houses on the left towards the walls of Brougham Hall ahead. The high walls and turrets are all that remain of the Hall built on the site of earlier fortified homes around 1830-40 by the first Lord Brougham and Vaux (see below). The Hall fell into disrepair and was demolished in 1934. The site is now undergoing restoration coupled with the development of craft workshops and other facilities. A notice board at the entrance gives further details.

> *The first Lord Brougham and Vaux, Henry Peter Brougham (1778-1868) was descended from an old Cumbrian family. He was born in Edinburgh and moved to London where he had a successful career as a lawyer before entering parliament, rising to become Lord Chancellor. Throughout his long career he was noted for his mental and physical energy – devoting his many talents and oratorical skills to the anti-slave trade movement, parliamentary reform, development of trade and education and other important causes. However, his overriding vanity and changing political stances did not endear him to some of his contemporaries.*

At the road junction, with Brougham Hall over the road in front of you, turn right and walk 100 metres to St Wilfred's Church **(F)**.

There is a notice on the door explaining that the key is available from the vicarage. The vicarage is about 400 metres down the road, which goes under the arch of the bridge connecting the church grounds with Brougham Hall.

After your visit, or external viewing (you can see inside through the plain glass windows on the north side) the walk continues on the road back to the vicarage (possibly for the second time for at least one of your party!). At the junction with the busy A6 turn right and cross the bridge over the River Lowther to walk towards Penrith with a stone wall and the river on your right. You pass the entrance to Lowther Holiday Park. There are two ancient monuments nearby. On the left is the earthwork, called, perhaps inappropriately, Arthur's Round Table, and details about this are given in the information board in the field. You need to make a detour if you wish to view the other, the Standing Stones at Maybrough Henge, which is about 500 metres away on the minor road which runs by Arthur's Round Table. The walk continues on the A6 past two pubs, The Crown on the left and The Beehive (dated 1727) on the right, to reach the river at Eamont Bridge **(G)**.

At the beginning of the road bridge there is a gate on the right, leading to a footbridge which enables pedestrians to cross the river in safety. Go across this footbridge and turn right by the sign indicating "Public Footpath to Brougham". In a few hundred metres, you reach a private property. Follow the public footpath, which turns to the left over a ladder stile then turns right over another ladder stile. Carry on through the trees. Effectively, the path takes you round the property and goes over another ladder stile to emerge in a field with the river on your right. Continue on the path which keeps to the line of the river as it bends and gets nearer to the busy A66. Penrith is over to the left. Where the river bends to the right, cross the stile and walk on along the field edge still following the line of the river. Subject to weather and the extent of foliage, the ruins of Brougham Castle, in the care of English Heritage with the English Heritage flag fluttering above, might be seen over the fields to the right. Carry on to cross another stile, after which the path comes closer to the river and is no longer separated from it by a fence. The path reaches a property, French Fields, where signs (and vociferous dogs) clearly indicate that the public footpath goes to the left. Follow the path as it skirts the boundary of the property and heads across the field to arrive at a ladder stile leading onto a disused road **(H)**.

Go over the style, turn right and walk 100 metres to join a minor road coming in on the left from the nearby busy A66. Turn right along this road and walk to the bridge over the River Eamont with Brougham Castle over to your right. Cross the bridge and proceed along the road to the entrance to Brougham Castle on your right **(I)**.

From the castle entrance walk in the same direction as before to come to a crossroads. Turn right to head back towards Brougham village. Continue walking along the road for 800 metres or so until you come to a junction. (The road to the left is the road you were on earlier when you left the "Church in the Barn"). Bear right and follow the road as it bears left to come to houses on your left with Brougham Hall at the top of the hill. Do not proceed all the way up the hill but take the first street on the left and, in 20 metres, at the junction, turn right and walk uphill. After about 200 metres come to a public footpath on your left **(J)**.

Take the public footpath which cuts across the corner of a private garden via two stiles to emerge onto a path between trees. Turn right and follow the path as it skirts below the gardens of the houses and leave it via a stile into a field. Walk slightly right aiming for the corner of the line of trees over to your right. The Clifton Pele Tower comes into view and is a good landmark to aim for as you cross the field to an arched gateway in the corner. The gateway is about 100 metres to the right of a small brick building. Go through the metal gate to arrive at a point where two minor roads join the A6. Bear left to walk on the pavement of this busy road for 800 metres to arrive back at Clifton Church and the end of the walk.

Walk 12(b), Clifton and Brougham omitting Brougham Castle: 5 miles

Follow Walk 12(a) as far as St Wilfred's Church **(F)**. After viewing the church, retrace your steps 100 metres back to the road junction and walk past the junction to take the first street on your left. Go down this street and look for a public footpath sign on your right then follow Walk 12(a) from **(J)**.

Walk 13: Greystoke

Lords, lecturers and livery

Location: St Andrew's Church, (NY443308) is in Greystoke, which is on the B5288, five miles west of Penrith.

Map: OS Outdoor Leisure 5: The English Lakes North Eastern area.

Distance: 5 miles

Terrain: The walk is on the level, mainly on public footpaths and quiet country roads.

Church: St Andrew, Greystoke.

Car parking: Parking is available near the church.

The Church

This is a large church – an impressive structure with an appearance of solidity and character. It is one of the biggest churches of medieval foundation in Cumbria. Historically, it is closely linked with the nearby Greystoke Castle and the Lords of Greystoke who have lived there from pre-conquest times. Since the 16th century, the Howard family (see below) has held the title.

Over many centuries, the church has been subject to several rebuilding and extension programmes, each of which has incorporated features from previous periods. Hence, although externally, the building looks to be of a similar style – possibly 17th century – there are many reminders of earlier work. Local legend has it that the reinstallation of the east window, as part of a major restoration in 1848, was not without its problems. Apparently, the glass had been removed and hidden as Cromwellian forces approached Greystoke in the 1640s. After 200 years, any parts missing were substituted with glass from other windows – with less than perfect results!

Once inside, there is an immediate sense that here you are in a really large church, with its wide nave leading to the long chancel and the great east window. The church guide gives an answer to the question "Why such a large building for a village the size of Greystoke?" Until the Reformation, there were three chapels on the north side of the nave and three on the south side. These had been endowed as chantry chapels – i.e. chapels where masses for the dead would be celebrated. Such chapels became unlawful and their furnishings and the screens dividing them from the nave were removed – leaving the vast wide nave you now see. The chancel was used by the monks of a medieval college centred at Greystoke and the stalls, some with misericords, in the long chancel would have been used by them.

In 1958, the educational tradition was revived, this time with the establishment of a pre-theological training college for prospective Church of England priests. It closed in 1979 owing to a fall in the number of applicants.

There are many interesting features to be seen at St Andrew's, ranging from the 13th-century supports for the chancel arch to 20th-century sculptures.

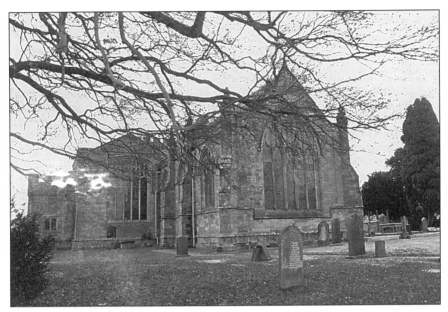

St Andrew, Greystoke, an impressive parish church

Among the other features of interest are:

❖ On the west wall, a figure of the crucified Christ, the work of the sculptress Josephina de Vasconcellos (see also Walk 24, St Mary and St Michael, Cartmel and Walk 29, St Mary the Virgin, Ambleside).

❖ At the west end, a wooden carving of the Madonna and child, made by three German prisoners of war, who were based at Greystoke Castle after the Second World War.

❖ The bestiary window, the oldest complete window in the church, on the south side of the chancel. This type of window depicts various animals and birds as part of Christian symbolism.

❖ The resurrection window, on the north wall near the organ, by Kempe (see Walk 8, All Saints, Bolton).

❖ On the north wall of the chancel in a recess, an alabaster effigy of John Lord Greystoke 16th Baron who died in 1436 together with a better preserved one of his grandfather William the 14th Baron. Also in the recess are memorials of the two colleges.

❖ The great east window which, despite the legend, presents an imposing focus behind the altar. The red devil is beneath the bishop's feet in the far left section. The glass in the tracery at the top is from the 19th century and incorporates the coats of arms of the Lords of Greystoke. The main panels are of medieval glass.

Information available in the church:

❶ A useful selection of literature including *The Story of St Andrew's Greystoke*, Canon David C. Ellis, updated 1996 by Revd Richard Frank

The Howard family succeeded the Greystokes, Grymethorpes and Dacres to become the fourth great house of Greystoke. The Dukes of Norfolk are Howards and two Dukes have lived in Greystoke Castle. Charles 11th Duke (1746-1815) extended Greystoke Park and built the enclosing wall that still exists. He also constructed four castellated farms, referred to by some commentators as folly-farms, near to the village. One fictional Lord of Greystoke is the hero of Edgar Rice Burrough's Tarzan of the Apes. In the book, Tarzan's birth name is revealed as John, Lord Greystoke. However, despite much speculation about a possible connection with the real Greystoke it seems that that Lord must remain in his novel domain.

The Walk

Leave the church **(A)** and grounds by the gateway at the west end and walk up the street. Immediately on your right is Spillers' Field where suicides were buried. A few metres further on, The Sanctuary Stone is displayed behind a metal grill set in the wall by the swimming pool. The Stone marked the spot beyond which fugitives could claim sanctuary. At the junction turn right, by the post office, and follow the road as it bears to the left round the Boot and Shoe pub. Over to your right, beyond the medieval village cross, is the entrance drive to Greystoke Castle. The road is signposted to Berrier. It leaves Greystoke passing Jefferson House, one of the farms built by the 11th Duke of Norfolk, on the left and goes through open farmland. Further on, on the right, is Greenthwaite Hall, which dates back to the 17th century. Carry straight on to Greystoke Moor Cottage beyond the beginnings of woodland on your right **(B)**.

Directly opposite the cottage is a sign indicating "Public Bridleway to Motherby". Cross the road and go through the gate to follow the broad track, which eventually takes a sharp turn to the right. Follow the track with a stone wall on your right as it passes through two gates. The path emerges onto an open grassy area. Keep walking in the same direction and go onto the broad track running between two field boundaries. Ahead there is wonderful mountain scenery, including Blencathra to the right. Keep to the track as it turns to the left and passes barns on the right before it arrives at the outskirts of Motherby village **(C)**.

Turn left and walk through the village, initially on a footpath but, as the houses are left behind, using the wide grass verge as appropriate. You might catch a glimpse of Greystoke church ahead. When the trees are bare, it appears, sentinel-like, overlooking fields in the distance. In about 800 metres from Motherby look out for a public bridleway post on your right and go through the wooden gate into the field. Bear left to go over the footbridge over the little burn then go through the gateway a few metres ahead. Keeping the wall on your right, proceed down towards a stream. Turn left as you

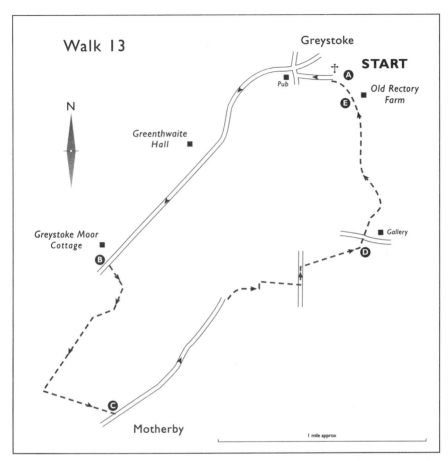

Walk 13

N

Greystoke

† **START**

Pub

Old Rectory
Farm

Greenthwaite
Hall ■

Greystoke Moor
Cottage ■

Ⓑ

■ Gallery

Ⓓ

Ⓒ

Motherby

1 mile approx

approach the stream, go through a wooden gate and turn right to cross the stream by the footbridge. Go through the gate ahead and keeping about 100 metres from the field boundary on your left go across the field and through a wooden enclosure to exit through the gates onto a minor road. Turn left and walk up the road the short distance to where it bends and, opposite a barn, take the track on the right. This track runs between hedges and, a little further on, alongside a stream on your left. It comes out at a minor road with a bridge over to your left **(D)**.

Cross the bridge and take the public footpath to Greystoke on your right. Initially this means walking up the drive towards the Gallery on your right. Where the drive bears to the right, go straight ahead across the grass to a stile. Go over the stile into a field and head straight across the field to a gateway beyond the telegraph post. Go through the gate and, turning very slightly right, walk across the field aiming for a point just to the left of the field corner to reach a gate (the second gate to the left of the stream). Go through the gate into the next field and walk along the field edge with the fence on your right. Cross the stile at end of the field, bear right and go over another stile. Turn left, and keeping the fence on your left, walk to the small red gate near to the buildings of Old Rectory Farm ahead (E).

The late Gordon W. Richards trained two Grand National winners from the stables here and his son now carries on the good work. To continue, take the public footpath to Greystoke, walking past a green building on your right to reach another gate. Go through this gate and along the field edge, with the fence on your right, through another gate, then through two small gates to cross a footbridge. Go through the gate at the end of the footbridge and walk ahead with the church and grounds on the right. The path arrives at a metal gate onto the road. On the right is the church and the end of the walk.

Walk 14: Martindale

Brows, boats and becks

Location: St Martin's (NY435184) is in Martindale on the south side of Ullswater. It is about 6 miles from Pooley Bridge on the minor road that passes the Sharrow Bay and Howtown hotels.

Distance: Walk 14(a), Martindale including Ullswater: 4½ miles; Walk 14(b), Martindale only: 2 miles.

Map: OS Outdoor Leisure 5: The English Lakes North Eastern area.

Terrain: These walks are almost entirely on public footpaths. Walk 14(a) includes some steep climbs.

Churches: St Martin of Tours, Martindale; St Peter, Martindale.

Car parking: There is parking outside both churches but the walks start from St Martin's which is about 800 metres beyond St Peter's.

The Churches

St Martin of Tours, Martindale

This church is generally referred to as the "Old Church of St Martin" or simply "St Martin's". The full dedication, however, is to St Martin of Tours, probably because of some connection with the influential northern missionary, St Ninian, who studied under St Martin at Tours in France.

The church stands in a very isolated location down in a valley about 800 metres south of its replacement, the "New Church of St Peter". From at least the early 13th century there was a church on this site, which was within the domain of the monks of Barton until the Dissolution of the Monasteries. The present building is believed to have been built towards the end of the 16th century, although there have been several restorations since that time, notably in 1882. This was the year in which the new church of St Peter was consecrated and when dramatically, as a result of a storm, the roof of St Martin's collapsed necessitating major repairs.

Subsequently, the church was used mainly for burials and, nowadays, it is only used on very special occasions. However, despite the obvious disappointment and inconvenience caused by thefts, the church is kept open and a notice proclaims that visitors are welcome here to "enjoy the simplicity and timeless atmosphere of this ancient place". This is indeed a church to take you back in time. It consists of a sparse single chamber of simple monastic appearance with its 17th-century pews positioned in their original sideways position. It is light and airy with exposed wooden roof beams and it has a stone flagged floor – an early 18th-century improvement when the earthern floor was replaced.

Among the other features of interest are:

❖ The font, believed to be of Roman origin, on which you can see groove marks probably as a result of sharpening tools.

❖ The plaque on the east wall in memory of William Dawes the last member of the family of that name from How Town, early patrons of this church.

❖ The reading desk (formerly a double-decker pulpit) dated 1634, a gift from a member of the Dawes family.

❖ The altar, engraved 1674, given in memory of Hilda Margaret Stanton from Sharrow Bay, who died in 1957, by her son.

❖ The yew tree by the north-east corner of the church which is believed to be about 700 years old. Under the tree is the large, bespattered tomb of the Revd George Woodley who is described as a missionary, an author and a poet.

❖ The tomb of the first post-reformation curate, Richard Birkett, outside the south-east corner of the church. He ministered here for almost 67 years and also acted as parish clerk, schoolmaster and moneylender. As was customary at the time, he enjoyed the benefits of "whittlegate", that is, free board and lodgings with his parishioners.

Information available in the church:

❶ A notice in the porch giving details of the history of the church.

❶ A leaflet, *The Churches in the Parish of Martindale.*

St Peter, Martindale

This is the "new" church which was built in the 1880s to replace St Martin's which, at that time, was considered to be too isolated for the parish of about 200 people in the scattered hamlet of Martindale. St Peter's now serves about 80 people and it stands in an extensive and well-kept churchyard at the top of the hause overlooking Ullswater, almost as isolated as its predecessor.

However, in striking contrast to the old church, it is clearly Victorian in style. Beneath the lofty ceiling there is a generous chancel which is almost as wide as the nave itself. There is an abundance of finely carved wood in evidence, notably in the choir stalls and in the reredos behind the altar. There are also several wall plaques in memory of benefactors and patrons, in particular to the Parkin family from Sharrow Bay who were responsible for the building of St Peter's in the first place.

It is perhaps the 20th century that now provides the most special feature of interest here. All the stained glass windows, apart from the east windows, date from 1975 and are the work of a contemporary artist and designer, Jane Grey. The events and personages depicted include: the Resurrection, the Ascension, St Patrick, St Ninian, St Cecilia and St Martin. The Queen's silver jubilee of 1977 is celebrated in three lancet windows in the north wall of the chancel. In the south wall of the nave, near to the chancel, there is a window in memory of Lieutenant Commander W H Parkin, the officers and men of *HMS Glorious*, which was sunk off Norway in 1940. Beside each window, there are helpful explanations which make interesting reading.

Information available in the church:

❶ A leaflet, *The Churches in the Parish of Martindale.*

The church of St Martin of Tours, nestling in the valley at Martindale

In sight of Ullswater at St Peter, Martindale

The Walks

Walk 14(a), Martindale including Ullswater: 4½ miles

Leave St Martin's churchyard **(A)**, turn right and walk back up the road. Ignore the footpath sign to the right shortly after the church but continue for about 300 metres before leaving the road to bear right through a gate marked "footpath" near a sign on the stone wall "Footpath to Howtown" **(B)**.

Climb gradually up the grassy track and go through a gateway. Skirt just below the boundary wall of Cotehow Cottages. Cross the track and continue up towards a wooden seat keeping the stone wall on the right. Take the opportunity to pause and appreciate Howgrain Beck below and a glimpse of Ullswater ahead. Follow the path uphill and through a gate. Then bear left, keeping close to a stone wall and some trees on your left, to make your way round to St Peter's Church **(C)**.

After visiting St Peter's, turn right to join the metalled road. Turn right again and walk up the road. Very soon, on reaching the highest point of the road, you will see a notice referring to the Dalemain Estates. Some 30 metres further on, leave the road to bear left onto a green path, which leads down to a low post indicating that cyclists have no right of way on the footpath. Now, as Ullswater comes more clearly into view with Howtown below on the right, you can relax and enjoy contouring around Hallin Fell on your left on the clear path. There are several old iron benches from which you can appreciate the extent of the lake, watch the yachts and the steamers, try to identify the famous Sharrow Bay Country House Hotel and admire the splendour of

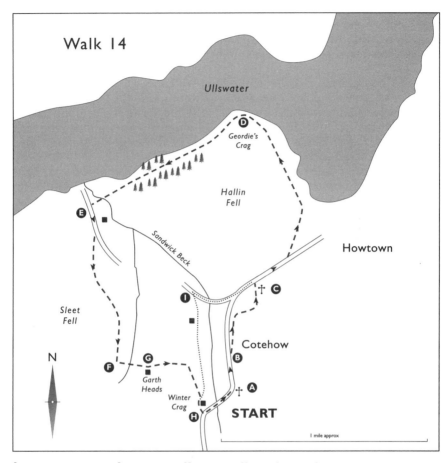

the tops to your right. Eventually you will need to pick your way more carefully over the rocks at the foot of Geordie's Crag (no connection with either of the authors!) **(D)**.

You then descend to the lakeside. Here you go through a kissing gate to enter Hallinhag Wood and you cross another short rocky section. Proceed for about 1200 metres on the main track through the pleasant wood, ignoring any paths off to the right, until you leave by a kissing gate. Continue on the clear path passing through four gates in short succession. A waymark on the railings then confirms you are on the right path! Continue for a further 100 metres and, when you reach the Sandwick Beck, turn left, and then soon go right to go over a bridge and through the gate at the far side. Ahead are some dwellings, including Bushby Cottage in the corner (planning permission to open a tea-room here was pending at the time of writing) **(E)**.

Turn left up the metalled road to pass Townhead Cottage on your right. Ignore the footpath to the right and also the bridlepath to Patterdale and continue on the road for a couple of hundred metres. Some 30 metres beyond a gateway of Millhow on the left, leave the road to bear right onto a grassy path through the ferns. You will see a number of paths visible ahead of you and you need to keep to the left on the lower path as you climb quite steeply to meet the top right-hand corner of the stone wall ahead. Proceed ahead keeping close to the wall on your left as you contour round the base of Sleet Fell. Resist the temptation to take any of the paths that invite you to climb steeply to the right! After a few hundred metres, when you are opposite the farm buildings of Garth Heads on the other side of the valley, watch out for a slightly concealed waymarked stile in the wall **(F)**.

Climb over and then cross another stile almost immediately on your right. Now bear left to descend to an old barn and a waymark sign. Follow the direction of the sign to bear right in front of a wall, through an open gateway and down to the beck. If you decide not to ford the beck, you can cross by the stone footbridge some 20 metres to the right. Then pick up the track which climbs gradually towards the farm buildings. Go over the stile next to the gate to pass Garth Heads on your right **(G)**.

Cross the metalled road and proceed straight ahead, noting the sign on the wall on your right which tells you the good news that you are heading towards Martindale. After going over the stile next to the public footpath sign, you then have a short but very steep ascent to complete. Continue up the grassy path, pausing for breath as needs must, until you reach a very conveniently placed bench at the top of the rise. Now you can enjoy the views of Ullswater and the two valleys. Ahead you should see your destination, Martindale Old Church. Descend on the path ahead between the crags, bearing right and keeping the wall on your left, to reach Winter Crag Farm and join a metalled road **(H)**.

Bear left and cross over the bridge to return to the church and the end of the walk.

Walk 14(b), Martindale only: 2 miles

Proceed as for Walk 14(a) as far as St Peter's Church **(C)**.

Leave St Peter's and turn right to join the metalled road. Now turn left and proceed downhill (Walk 14(a) goes uphill at this point). At the road junction bear right in the direction signposted to Sandwick. Cross the bridge over the beck and about 200 metres further on take a sharp left turn off the road onto a track which doubles back from the road **(I)**.

Follow the track past the cottage on your right and then continue on the green path with the wall on your left eventually to reach the buildings of Winter Crag Farm where you join the metalled road **(H)**.

Bear left and cross over the bridge to return to the church and the end of the walk.

Walk 15: Wreay

Remembrance, railway and riverbanks

Location: St Mary's Church (NY435489) is in Wreay, which is 5 miles south-east of Carlisle.

Map: OS Outdoor Leisure 5: The English Lakes North Eastern area.

Distance: 3½ miles.

Terrain: Mainly on the level on public footpaths with one short section on a main road.

Church: St Mary, Wreay.

Car parking: There is parking on the roadside near St Mary's Church.

The Church

The church of St Mary, Wreay, is unique. According to Simon Jenkins (*England's Thousand Best Churches*) "This one of the most eccentric small churches in England". Expect some surprises when you visit this church.

The present building was consecrated in 1842. A church on the site had been built in the 14th century. That church was probably replaced by another building, which was consecrated in1719, and which also served as a school. By the late 1830s, this second church was in a dilapidated state. The present church was built as its replacement by Miss Sarah Losh. She designed and paid for the building. Her motivation was to make a lasting memorial in

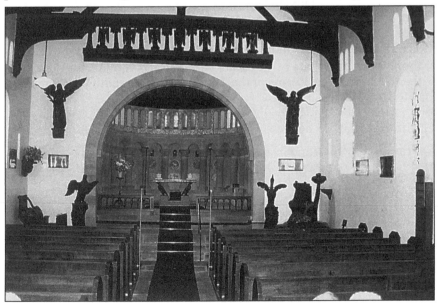

The surprising interior of St Mary, Wreay *(with the kind permission of the vicar)*

remembrance of her sister Catherine, who died young in 1835, and of her parents.

From the outside the church is seen as a small rectangular building with a sloping roof and a large apse. At the west end is a bellcote surmounted by a stone eagle. Under the eaves at each corner are large monster gargoyles. In combination these features give the church an unusual external appearance.

Entry into the church is through the west door. Once inside the real surprises come. There is a complete mixture of styles in both the architecture and furnishings. The underlying concepts behind them are partly derived from Miss Losh's travels in Europe, particularly in Italy, but developed by her in imaginative and innovative ways. There is certainly much to appreciate in this place.

Whether the 1840s' congregations found the building and its ornamentations to their taste is not known. Today at Wreay there is a regular worshipping community, which welcomes visitors to this "different" church.

Among the other features of interest are:

❖ The portrait of Miss Losh on the west wall as you come in.

❖ The alabaster font, in the south-west corner as you enter, with ten panels carved by Sarah Losh and the cover with lotus flowers by her cousin William Losh. The various decorations, including Norman zig-zag and Greek fluting, demonstrate a mixture of styles – almost a Wreay tradition!

❖ The small upper windows of the nave each with three little sections of bright, attractive stained glass.

❖ The pulpit made from the stump of a hollow oak with the nearby candle holder in the shape of a palm tree.

❖ The altar table of green Italian marble and supported by two brass eagles.

❖ In the apse, an arcade of 14 pillars with 13 seats in the spaces between them. Above are emblems of the 12 apostles surrounding the lamb, the emblem of Christ.

❖ In the church grounds the mausoleum which is a memorial to Catherine Losh and contains an alabaster seated figure of her.

Information available in the church:

❶ A leaflet, *St Mary's Church Wreay.*

The Walk

Leave the church **(A)** by the west door, bear right and walk round the building and continue beyond the east end on a path of paving stones through the church grounds to come out on a road. This is the Carlisle road. Turn left and walk a short distance to a public footpath sign "Newbiggin" on your right. Take this metalled lane and follow it to cross a railway (the main Glasgow to London line). Just beyond the next bend go over the stile on your right. The stile has a yellow waymark and is topped by metal hoops. Walk downhill, keeping close to the fence on your right towards the river, going over another

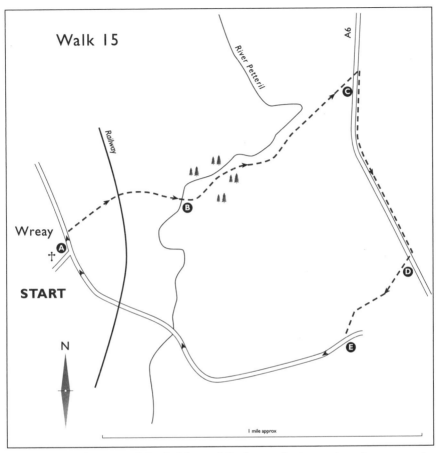

Walk 15

River Petteril

A6

C

Railway

Wreay

†

A

START

B

D

E

N

1 mile approx

stile. Near the bottom of the field, a public footpath sign points the way to the left. Walk in the direction indicated, skirting the copse of trees on your right, to arrive at a metal footbridge over the River Petteril. Cross the bridge, turn left and walk to the wood ahead. Go over the stile into the wood **(B)**.

Follow the path through the woods. At one point the path goes through a gate near to which there is a notice board pointing out that these woods are owned and managed by the Cumbria Wildlife Trust. When the footpath begins to climb, it divides. Take the right-hand waymarked path to go up the steps. At the top go over the stile to emerge into a field **(C)**.

Go straight ahead towards a road with the grounds and buildings of Scaleshaugh on your left. Pass through the kissing gate, cross the road and go through a similar kissing gate. Walk straight up the field, with Scaleshaugh grounds still on the left, to reach a gate. Go through the gate to arrive at the A6 road. Usually, this section of the A6 is less busy than it is further south but most vehicles travel at a fast speed. Hence, take care as you cross to the pavement on the other side. Turn right and walk along the pavement for just over 800 metres. Look out for a public footpath sign on the other side of the road and, with care, go over the road to this sign **(D)**.

Go through the gate onto the public footpath. Walk straight ahead with the hedgerow and wire fence on your right. Follow the field boundary to come to a gate. Go through the gate and bear left to walk 10 metres to another gate. Go through this gate and turn right to walk up the field with a fence on your right towards a barn. Bear left and walk along the side of the barn (which is on your right). At the end of the barn bear slightly right and walk up the field to exit via a gate onto a minor road **(E)**.

Turn right to walk the final mile back to Wreay along this delightful country road. After about 300 metres or so the road bears right. You walk alongside a wood on your left and pass an entrance to Wreay Hall on your right. The road crosses the River Petteril at Wreay Bridge and you go through a little hamlet with some interesting properties. Follow the road as it passes underneath the main Glasgow to London railway line and in a short while enters Wreay village, with the Plough Inn on the right and, on the left, the church and the end of the walk.

Walk 16: Wythburn

*Outpost of deanery, tracks through greenery and
"aerial" scenery*

Location: Wythburn Church (NY324136) is on the A591 Grasmere to Keswick road
just above Thirlmere, 3½ miles north of Grasmere.

Distance: Walk 16(a), Thirlmere and Harrop Tarn: 4½ miles; Walk 16(b), Thirlmere
only: 3 miles.

Map: OS Outdoor Leisure 5: The English Lakes North Eastern area.

Terrain: The walks are on footpaths and forest tracks with short sections on a quiet
minor road. Walk 16(a) involves some steep ascents and descents while Walk 16(b)
is on the level.

Church: Wythburn Church.

Car parking: There is generous car parking behind the church.

The Church

Wythburn Church is a relatively small isolated valley chapel, set into the
hillside beneath the Helvellyn range and separated by a road from the shores
of Thirlmere. The church guidebook aptly describes it as "rather like a
stranded boat without an ocean to sail on, or a crew". Although it now serves
a mere handful of houses, this was not always the case. Prior to the conversion of Thirlmere into a reservoir to supply the needs of Manchester towards
the end of the 19th century, the Nag's Head stood opposite and the Cherry

Wythburn Church beneath the Helvellyn range

Tree was a little further north, both staging posts for the horse-drawn coaches which plied between Keswick and Grasmere. Wythburn also boasted its own post office and other dwellings now long submerged beneath the encroaching waters of the reservoir. Near to Dunmail Raise, it was the first (or the last) church in the old County of Cumberland and now it stands on the fringe of Derwent Deanery

The church was built in 1640 on the site of a chapel of 1554. It was always simple and humble and Wordsworth in *The Waggoner*, written in 1805, referred to it as a "modest house of prayer". Today you find the white rendered rectangular nave with deeply recessed windows much as it would have appeared in Wordsworth's time, before the addition of the slate chancel, apse and vestry in 1872.

Visitors are made to feel welcome here, even to the extent of a welcome notice on the hymn board. There is seating for about 100 people in the narrow nave, which leads to the semi-circular apse with its exposed wooden rafters, behind which are three small stained glass windows. These windows, like those in the west wall, are dedicated to the Revd Basil Lawson, who served here for 43 years. On the south wall there are two war memorials, otherwise the walls are pleasantly devoid of ornamentation.

Despite being so close to the main road, the grounds are pleasant and tranquil. Two very tall conifers provide useful landmarks on the walks and additional land and trees were added by North West Water to commemorate the centenary of the reservoir in 1979.

Among the other features of interest are:

❖ The finely carved communion rails.

❖ The wheelbarrow in the chancel! Formerly owned by Manchester Corporation Water Works and on loan from St John-in-the-Vale Church.

❖ The west window showing St Cuthbert (with the head of St Oswald), Christ the King and St Heribert (also spelt Herbert or Herebert) of Derwentwater.

Information available in the church:

❶ A notice on the south wall opposite the entrance with a brief history of the church.

❶ *The Parishes of St John's-in-the-Vale and Wythburn*, Geoffrey Darrall.

The Walks

Walk 16(a), Thirlmere and Harrop Tarn: 4½ miles

After visiting the church **(A)** return to the car park and follow the drive that leads back towards the main road. Just before the main road go through a kissing gate on the left onto the permissive path to Homestead Green, Dunmail and Grasmere. Now follow this path as it takes you a short distance through the wood and across a number of footbridges, ignoring a path off to the right, before the main path re-enters the wood and widens out into a clear

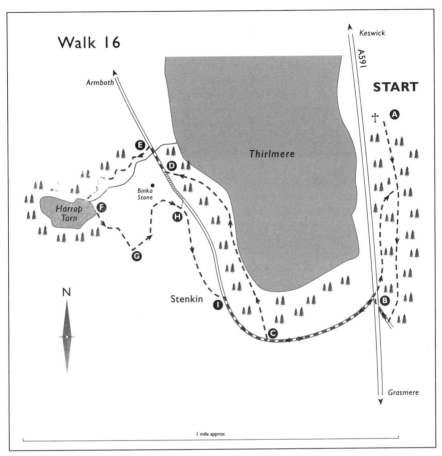

Walk 16

Keswick

A591

START

Armboth

Thirlmere

Binka Stone

Harrop Tarn

N

Stenkin

Grasmere

1 mile approx

forest track. After passing through two gates you join a wider track. Turn right and descend to cross a stile next to a gate to meet the main road**(B)**.

Cross the busy road with care and continue along the road, opposite, in the direction of Armboth for about 800 metres to Steel End car park**(C)**.

Go through the car park and pass through a gate to take the permissive lakeshore footpath to Dobgill. Several white waymarks indicate the path ahead. After the second and third waymarks open views across the lake reveal Wythburn Church with the two tall conifers in the grounds. Follow the path which passes over some duck boarding (which can be slippery) and go through the small gate until the path eventually leads you back onto the road via a kissing gate **(D)**.

Turn right and proceed just over 100 metres to Dobgill car park and toilets **(E)**.

Take the path in the left-hand corner of the car park by the noticeboard. Climb the steps, go through the high kissing gate and continue up the steep stony path to zig-zag up from the road. The path is clear which is just as well because the forest is dark, and it takes you past some high crags on your left and then emerges back into the open just before the Dobgill waterfalls. After passing through a clearing you suddenly encounter the delightful Harrop Tarn **(F)**.

Turn left and cross a footbridge. Now continue round the side of the tarn for a short way to exit through a high wooden gate on the left where the fence begins. Bear right and climb gradually away from the tarn on the grassy path with the wall on your right. When the wall bears off to the right take a narrow path straight ahead through the bracken to the top of the rise Another good excuse to rest and admire the "aerial" view of Thirlmere and over the lake to Wythburn Church **(G)**.

Turn right and walk straight ahead along the rise, passing a small cairn on your left and then bear slightly right to descend towards a broken wall with two stiles behind. Do not go through the broken wall, but instead turn left and descend on the grassy path, keeping close to the wall on your right. Continue downhill for a few hundred metres and make for a small plateau ahead with a large boulder on top. Wythburn Church is visible ahead in the distance. As the church momentarily disappears from view, leave the wall to bear left on a grassy path, passing the plateau on your right. You are now heading in the direction of the huge Binka Stone, which stands just above the road below. The path becomes very stony and care is needed over a relatively short section before resuming on a gentler green path. You then go down more gradually and about 150 metres before the Binka Stone bear right to make towards a gate in the wall just before the road. Do not go through this gate (this is where the Walk 16(b) rejoins the route). About 10 metres before the gate, turn right onto a path which is somewhat faint at first **(H)**.

The path continues ahead with a wall and the road parallel below you on your left. It takes you through two gates and past some ruined dwellings and a fingerpost before descending gradually to meet the road after passing through the gates and yard of Stenkin **(I)**.

Now turn right and follow the road back past Steel End car park to the main road. Cross the busy road with care and take the helpful footpath "Wythburn Church to avoid road" on the left through the gate. Make your way back along the narrow path, which joins a wider track. Bear left and retrace your steps back to the church and the end of the walk.

Walk 16(b), Thirlmere only: 3 miles

Follow the main walk as far as **(D)**. Turn left along the road and proceed for a few hundred metres, passing below the huge Binka Stone up on your right. Leave the road via a gate on your right by a bridleway sign to Watendlath. Climb a short way on the grassy track to go through a waymarked gate. Bear left, ignoring the bridleway to your right, to rejoin Walk 16(a) from **(H)** above.

Walk 17: Bootle and Corney

Connection, climb and coast views

Location: St Michael and All Angels (SD108884) is in Bootle on the A595.

Map: OS Outdoor Leisure 6: The English Lakes South Western area.

Distance: Walk 17(a), Bootle and Corney: 10½ miles; Walk17(b), Bootle only: 6 miles.

Terrain: Mainly on public footpaths and minor roads with one short section on a busier fell road. Both walks include one long gradual ascent.

Churches: St Michael and All Angels, Bootle; St John the Baptist, Corney.

Car parking: There is a car park on the left-hand side of the road opposite the church.

The Churches

St Michael and All Angels, Bootle

This church is an impressive redstone building, cruciform in shape with a sturdy west tower. It is on the busy A595, which carries heavy traffic through Bootle village and is better viewed from a short distance away in order to appreciate its handsome exterior.

The ancestry of the building has not been exactly determined but it has Norman masonry in the nave. Much of what is now seen dates from Victorian reconstructions. The transepts are from 1837 and the tower from about

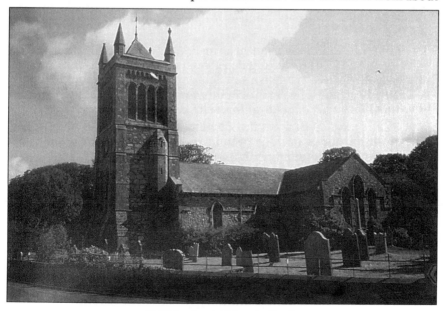

St Michael and All Angels, Bootle

1860-1880 and it is probable that the arched entrances to the transepts also date from then.

Entry is through the west door into the porch area at the base of the tower and through glass doors into the nave. In front of you is a long nave, leading to a chancel arch with arched bays at the entrances to the transepts and a chancel with carved oak choir stalls. Overhead is a very high ceiling with heavy exposed beams and elaborate brass paraffin lamps, now tastefully converted to electricity. Bearing in mind that the church was completely reconstructed in Victorian times, and possibly contrary to one's expectations, there is not an excess of memorial tablets and only a limited amount of stained glass.

This is a large building. It easily accommodates its furnishings and memorials without overcrowding. Instead there is a feeling of cohesiveness and holiness.

Among the other features of interest are:

❖ The stone font on its large plinth and with its elaborate, carved "witches hat" cover. The font is thought to be 16th century but there is some doubt as to its antiquity.

❖ The long embroidered pew cushions.

❖ The stained glass windows in the north and south transepts – even if only to see whether you agree with Pevsner's view that they are terrible!

❖ The tablet on the south wall of the south transept setting out the extra seating, including "free places", made available by the 1837 extensions. The practice of allocating pew numbers to specific families was subsequently abolished.

❖ On the south wall of the chancel a small brass tablet to Sir Hugh Askew who died in 1562. He was knighted at the Battle of Musselburgh in1547 – the last battle between English and Scots in the Border disputes. He lived at Seaton Hall, one mile north of Bootle, awarded to him at the time of the Reformation for his exploits at Musselburgh and elsewhere.

St John the Baptist, Corney

Corney Church stands on high ground in an exposed position but with extensive views all around. Conditions permitting, the Isle of Man is visible from the well cared for graveyard. It is on the site of an earlier church, which possibly dates back to the 12th century. The date of construction of the present building is not known. Most of what is now seen is the result of a restoration in 1882, but there are traces of older styles, in particular the doorways in the west end and on the north wall of the chancel.

Inside, there are plain walls, exposed roof beams and solid pews; in addition, a chancel arch and choir stalls. The oil lamps have been tastefully converted to electricity. The font is from 1882. There is only one memorial tablet, which is to Joseph Benn, a native of Corney who died in 1860. He served 42 years as agent to the Earls of Lonsdale (see Walk 10: St Michael, Lowther).

Hill top isolation at St John the Baptist, Corney

The very simplicity of the place does not lead to an expectation of a long list of specific features of interest. Sadly, there are fewer items of interest here now, since, in January 2000, three of the church's sundials were stolen.

At the west end, a crude wooden cross is attached to the roof beams. This, perhaps, helps to engender the feeling of sanctity that is present in these simple churches as much as in grander places.

The Walks

Walk 17(a), Bootle and Corney: 10½ miles

Leave the church (A) and grounds by the gate onto the main A595. Cross the busy road with care and walk along the pavement by the main road through the village as far as the Evangelical Church.

Bootle Evangelical Church was founded in 1780 by John Whitbridge of London, who was associated with a religious body called the Countess of Huntington's Connection. The church has always maintained a level of independence; it was a Congregational church and for a short time, following the amalgamation of the Congregational and Presbyterian Churches, a United Reformed Church. It is supported in its work of maintaining an evangelical presence in the area by the Rural Ministries organisation.

Cross the A595 to the narrow metalled road opposite. Walk along this road and continue as it climbs, passing a number of properties, for about a mile. Shortly after passing Fellgate Cottage, leave the main track and continue straight ahead, past a stone barn to a gate. The waymark indicates that you are going onto a public bridleway and footpath **(B)**.

Go through the gate onto the well-defined track You are on the track, which is easy to follow, for the next couple of miles as it gradually ascends Bootle Fell and skirts to the left of Stoneside Hill ahead. Within a mile you arrive at the Resting Stone which is a good place for a rest but which takes its name from the manner in which it is positioned. Apart from the magnificent fell views all around, take the opportunity to look back to enjoy seeing the sea in the distance. As you near Stoneside Hill cross the stile onto a metalled section and follow this, with the summit above you on your right, to come to a busier fell road **(C)**.

Having climbed up to this point you can now benefit from a downhill section. Turn left and proceed along the road for about 1200 metres to Buckbarrow Bridge. This road can be quite busy at times so watch out for speeding vehicles especially round bends. After the bridge carry on uphill for about 350 metres and just before the brow, opposite to where a path comes in from the right, take the path on the left. There is no footpath sign. The path is indistinct and there are boggy sections to be negotiated. Bear slightly left towards the gully of the Kinmont Beck, aiming for the farmhouse ahead among the trees by the side of the beck. Pick up a green path, which takes you along the ridge with the beck below on your left. A stone wall appears ahead and you need to aim for its left-hand corner. Go through the gate in the wall **(D)**.

Walk straight ahead with the beck on your left and the wall on your right. As the wall bears right continue ahead towards the farm buildings and about 200 metres before the farm bear left to the beck. Here there is a ford and a bridge with a notice that it a private bridge restricted to agricultural traffic. Cross the beck and bear right to follow the green track as it climbs to a gate. Go through the gate and walk with a wall on your left to another gate. Go through this gate into woods and keep on the path through the woods to exit via a gate to a footbridge. Cross the footbridge and turn left to follow the path to exit via a gate onto a minor road **(E)**.

Turn right and walk up this minor road, passing Low Kinmont on the right and Spring House on the left. Just beyond Spring House, Corney Church comes into view ahead on the left. A few hundred metres later take the public footpath "Corney Hall" on the left. Go over the stone stile and proceed along the field boundary with the wire fence and hedge on your right to a stile. Cross the stile and go down the steep bank with the fence on your left. Carry on past trees on your left to a gate. Go through the gate and bear right across the field to cross a footbridge **(F)**.

Turn right and walk to a gate leading to a wood. Go through the gate and follow the path through the wood – the path is overgrown in parts – to exit via a gate onto a farm road. Turn right and go along the road past a house on the right to come to a junction with a metalled road. Turn left and walk up the

Walk 17

steep hill to arrive at the entrance gate to Corney Church grounds on your left **(G)**.

Leave the church and retrace your steps down the hill, along the farm road and through the wood to the footbridge **(F)**.

Instead of crossing the footbridge, carry straight on to Corney Hall farm ahead. Proceed through the farm area, via the farm gates, passing the farmhouse on your left. Exit the area by the farm road going out from the right-hand corner. Continue along the road with a copse on your left. At the end of the copse leave the farm road by a track on your left to a gate about 15 metres ahead. Go through the gate and turn left to walk along the field boundary with a wall on your left and, ignoring the gate on your left, keep straight ahead to go through a gate into the next field. Carry on in the same direction aiming for a gate that is 50 metres or so from the left-hand corner of the field. Go through the metal kissing gate, then bear diagonally right, and proceed towards the stone wall, aiming for a gate just to the right of the farm buildings at Seaton Hall. Go through he kissing gate to walk to another gate and exit onto a farm road. Cross this and the bridge opposite and go via a couple of gates into a field **(H)**.

Behind the wall over to the left you might catch a glimpse of the ruins of Seaton Hall priory. A Benedictine nunnery, one of only two in Cumbria, was established here in the late 12th century but the buildings and grounds were ceded to Sir Hugh Askew at the time of the Reformation. Continue in the same direction with trees on your left. Keep walking straight ahead over four fields with their corresponding gateways and with the wire fence and old wall boundaries on your left to emerge via a gate onto a minor road. Turn right and walk to the junction with the busy A595 **(I)**.

Taking care, cross the road and take the footpath to the left of the cottages opposite. Walk past the houses to come to a gate. Go through this, follow the clear lonnen for 800 metres or so, and exit via a gate onto a track with houses nearby. Walk the few metres to a junction. Turn left and keep on this road for 800 metres back to the church and the end of the walk.

Walk 17(b), Bootle only: 6 miles
Follow the directions for Walk 17(a) as far as **(E)**.

Turn left and walk along the minor road to its junction with the A595. Then follow the directions for Walk 17(a) from **(I)** to return to the church and the end of the walk.

Walk 18: Coniston and Torver
Reformer, record-breaker and a "road"

Location: St Andrew's Church (SD303976) is in Coniston, 7½ miles south-west of Ambleside on the A593 Ambleside to Broughton in Furness road.

Distance: 8 miles.

Map: OS Outdoor Leisure 6: The English Lakes South Western area.

Terrain: The walk is almost entirely on footpaths and well-defined tracks. It is largely on the level but there are a number of sections involving steady but not steep climbs and descents. If desired, the climbs can be avoided altogether by retracing your steps from Torver back along the shore of Coniston Water.

Churches: St Andrew, Coniston; St Luke, Torver.

Car parking: There are several pay and display car parks in Coniston. The most convenient is about 150 metres past the church on the right-hand side. This also contains a Lake District National Park Information Centre and toilets.

The Churches

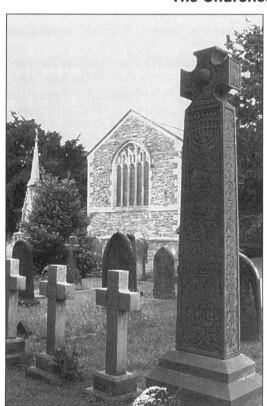

The Ruskin Memorial at St Andrew, Coniston

St Andrew, Coniston

The church stands very centrally in present day Coniston and as such must be seen, if not visited, by practically every incoming tourist. It nearest neighbours cater for the influx of visitors with offerings of postcards, souvenirs and groceries.

Although it is believed that there was a chapel here as early as the 12th century significant records only remain of the chapel built in 1586 by the Le Fleming family of Coniston Hall (see also Walk 27, St Oswald, Grasmere).

Coniston grew in size in the 19th century with the exploitation of the copper mines, the slate quarries and the advent of the railway. Not surprisingly, therefore, this was reflected in the growth of the village and the development of the church.

The Elizabethan chapel was replaced by a new chapel in 1819 and this, in turn, was substantially restored and almost totally refurbished in 1891. It is largely the latter that you see today.

The building is spacious, light and airy with a high ceiling supported by well-proportioned timber beams bearing a simple motif. This is clearly an active place of worship with the walls adorned with interesting displays at the time of writing. The rear of the church has been made into a meeting space with the imaginative use of millennium funding and the conversion of surplus oak pews into cupboards.

The only surviving item from the early period of the church is the wall plaque in memory of Alice Fleming in the south-east wall. The epitaph makes particularly interesting reading and the complete text is reproduced in the church guidebook.

Among the other features of interest are:

❖ The west window, located in the baptistry, designed by Kempe (see Walk 8 All Saints, Bolton). An interesting and magnified view of this window can be seen reflected in the glass screen from the rear of the church.

❖ The tablet of 1757, to the right of the north doorway, which gives details of church funding.

❖ The memorials on the left wall of the chancel arch and especially the story of James Hewitson V.C. whose gravestone stands outside the west door.

❖ The east window in memory of William and Sarah Barratt, members of the Barratt family, originally from Cornwall, promoters of the copper mines and generous patrons of Coniston (see below, St Luke, Torver).

❖ The grave of John Ruskin (see below) which stands in the north-east corner of the churchyard. The memorial cross was designed by his secretary W.G. Collingwood, a noted writer and artist in his own right, who lies buried nearby (see also Walk 27, St Michael and All Angels, Hawkshead).

Information available in the church:

❶ *The Parish of Church Coniston "St Andrew"*, D. Butterworth.

❶ *John Ruskin in Coniston*, John Dawson.

St Luke, Torver

St Luke's stands at the north-east end of the small and scattered hamlet of Torver. Apparently it is the third church which has stood on this site since the 12th century. A simple dales church was demolished in 1849 and its replacement was pulled down in 1884 when the present church was built and dedicated to St Luke.

It is a good example of a late 19th-century church, described in the church booklet as being designed "out of a textbook". The interior is neat and intimate with a narrow nave leading to the chancel through two arches. The arches serve as supports for the substantial tower.

There are relatively few wall tablets and dedications. However, not surprisingly, the Barratts of Coniston, the major landowners in Torver in the

St Luke, Torver, and conveniently adjacent inn

19th century, are remembered in the east and west windows, dedicated to William and Sarah Barratt respectively (see also above, St Andrew's Church).

The Revd Thomas Ellwood was vicar here from 1861 to 1911 and there are windows bearing his name and that of his wife Dorcas in the chancel. In addition to overseeing the construction of St Luke in 1883-84, the Revd Ellwood was responsible for the building of the adjacent school, now village hall, and for leaving a lot of details about the church and Torver in his book *Forty-five years in a Mountain Parish.*

Although this church is generally locked, apart from when it is used for services, arrangements for people to visit the church are detailed on the door. In any event, the attractive window given by the children of the parish in 1913 is worth viewing in the porch.

Among the other features of interest are:

❖ The sandstone font thought to be of the 14th century.

❖ The texts on the west wall.

❖ The plaque dated 1729, on the south wall, referring to a gift from a mariner from Whitehaven to pay for learning and books for the poor.

Information available in the church:

❶ *The Three Churches of Torver,* J. Dawson and C.F. Smith.

The Walk

After visiting St Andrew's Church **(A)**, leave by the main gate and turn left to go over the bridge on the road signposted to Broughton and Ulverston and follow the road as it bears left past a garage. Just after crossing the junction with Station Road a raised pavement on the right-hand side takes you past Coniston Methodist Church which dates from 1875. The chapel is generally only open for services but you can see that it is well cared for within its small neat grounds. Cross over the road to continue along the pavement, which is now on the other side, for a few hundred metres and take the stile on the left onto the public footpath **(B)**.

According to the guidebook to St Andrew's Church, this stile was known as "Priest's Stile" because it was frequently used by the curate on his visits to Coniston Hall, your immediate destination. From the stile you can glimpse the white buildings of John Ruskin's home at Brantwood across the northern end of Coniston Water.

John Ruskin (1819-1900) was a man of many parts who enjoyed international fame as an artist, an art critic, a poet and a social reformer. He was also responsible for initiating the local craft of making the intricately patterned "Ruskin" lace. He had enjoyed family holidays in the Lake District and, when the opportunity arose, he enthusiastically exchanged life in London for the peace and quiet of Brantwood, overlooking Coniston Water and Coniston Fells. Perhaps not surprisingly he asked to be buried in Coniston rather than in Westminster Abbey where his reputation would certainly have merited him a final resting place. Brantwood is open to the public and is well worth a visit as is the Ruskin Museum in Coniston Village itself.

Follow the clear path in the direction of the waymark to cross a ladder stile. Go through a kissing gate. To your right look out for the Sacred Heart R.C. Church (1872) at Bowmanstead to which Ruskin generously donated a window. Sadly, at the time of writing, the church was locked outside of service times due to burglary. Ahead are the four chimneys of Coniston Hall. A wider surfaced track leads you to the metalled road, which passes the sailing club and the hall (now the property of the National Trust). Just beyond the vehicular barrier follow the sign, "Footpath to Torver", our next destination. Shortly a sign on a kissing gate tells you that you are on the Cumbria Way. Keep on the metalled road through the campsite and, at a fork, continue in the same direction passing a yellow waymark. When you are about 150 metres from the far boundary wall, take a waymarked track on the left that leaves the road to go towards the lake to the left of a plantation. Soon you are through a gate and by the lakeshore. Continue along the shoreline, through some gates, to a Lake District National Park sign for Torver Commons, just beyond a boathouse and a jetty. This is a good spot from which to appreciate the straight unimpeded nature of Coniston Water.

Coniston Water is 5 miles long and was therefore a suitable venue for Donald Campbell to attempt to set water speed records. Sadly, of course, it was here on Coniston that he lost his life in his boat "Bluebird" in 1967 when trying to establish a record in excess of 300 mph. There are plaques in memory of

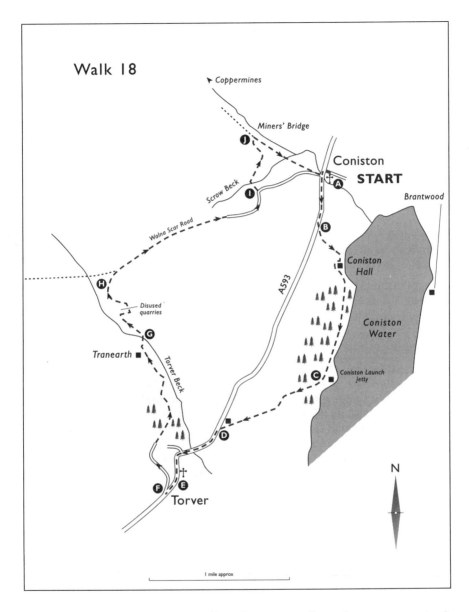

Donald Campbell and his chief mechanic Leo Villa on the green opposite the public car park, not far from the church. More information can be found in the Ruskin Museum in Coniston village. The speed of "Bluebird" contrasts with the leisurely pace of Arthur Ransome's tale, "Swallows and Amazons", based on this area.

Now proceed ahead on the clear track at the edge of the wood. Pass a yellow waymark, cross a beck and to your left is a jetty for the Coniston Launch. Some 100 metres beyond, as you enter a clearing in the woods, there is a low footpath sign "Torver" which you need to follow off to the right **(C)**.

Follow the green path, with a broken wall on your right, and stay with it as it ascends to become a stony track leading up through the pleasant woods. Eventually after passing through two gates you leave the wood at some ruined buildings, and the buildings of Brackenbarrow Farm appear ahead with the rugged heights of Coniston Old Man clearly in view to the right. The clear track leads to a stile and after a few hundred metres you cross a minor road to take a stile next to the gate directly opposite. Here a public footpath sign reassures you that you are on the right path. Follow the grassy path, which may be boggy in parts, as it bears right to cross a stile just beyond a broken wall. You now cross the disused railway which once served the local mines, and then some duck boarding, after which you bear right to go through a metal kissing gate next to a wooden gate to exit onto the A593 at Brigg House **(D)**.

Turn left, taking care with the traffic, and walk a few hundred metres to arrive at St Luke's Church **(E)**.

After visiting the church continue along the road, passing Church House Inn, for a further 150 metres or so until you arrive at the Wilson Arms where you take the public footpath signposted off to the right of the pub **(F)**.

Follow the track through the wooden gate and climb gradually up the narrow walled path as it winds its way below the white house on the hillside ahead, ignoring gates off to the left and right. Eventually the path broadens out and bears right as it joins a metalled road. Climb more steeply to meet a junction at Scarr Head Caravan and Campsite and follow the road as it bears left, passing a low post indicating "Public Bridleway Walna Scar". Now continue to ascend as the road becomes more of a stony track. Go through a gate and, after skirting the edges of the woodlands of High Torver, Coniston Old Man comes back into view. Eventually you pass through a second gate at an old building and, after about 50 metres, the path bears right in the direction of a bridleway sign that also refers to Tranearth (a former climbing hut, now a National Trust property). Continue along the track passing through a couple of gates before bearing right to go over a stream. Tranearth is over to the left and the spoil of the old slate quarry can be seen ahead. Go through a small waymarked gate and then almost immediately through another gate on the right as the path takes you across a footbridge over the Torver Beck **(G)**.

Follow the path as it bears left upstream (ignoring a bridleway path off to the right) and through the quarry waste. A waterfall becomes visible as the clear stony path bears round the top of the old quarry. Continue ascending on the main track above the quarry and, after a few hundred metres, with the beck clearly visible on the left, the track divides. Take the right fork and you will soon find a number of grassy paths ahead that lead to the popular track known as the Walna Scar Road. The far right-hand side path is probably your best route to this clear stony "road" **(H)**.

Now proceed along the clear track eventually to pass a parking area where you go through a metal gate and onto a metalled road. Walk down the road and at a sharp bend, by a gravel turning space and access to a fenced utility, leave the road to take a slightly concealed stile in the corner, just beyond a public footpath sign, "Miners' Bridge; Coppermines Valley" **(I)**.

(On the other hand, if you are weary at this stage this is a convenient cut-off point. You can continue straight down the road to Coniston and save yourself 1 mile!)

To continue, keeping close to the wall on your right, proceed ahead to pass through a kissing gate and then descend to go through a gate. Turn left and cross a footbridge over Scrow Beck. Bear right through the bracken to join a grassy path with the wall again on your right. Follow the clear path as it winds its way round the base of the crag on your left Eventually some dwellings appear up the valley, remnants of the days when the area was famous for its copper mines. A Youth Hostel and the Coppermines Valley Heritage Centre now attract visitors there. The path descends to a junction just before the strongly flowing Church Beck and Miners' Bridge **(J)**. (Your path today is not across the bridge but it is a good vantage point nevertheless).

Turn right and follow the broad track down with the steam on your left, keeping to the clear path until it eventually takes you onto a road at Dixon Ground Farm. Proceed ahead past the cottages and turn left at the Sun Inn. Walk down the lane in front of the pub. The tower of St Andrew's Church soon comes into view and you cross the bridge that brings you back to the church and the end of the walk.

Walk 19: Eskdale
"L'aal Ratty" sights, tarn on the heights, funereal rites

Location: St Catherine's Church, Eskdale (NY176003) is on the outskirts of the small hamlet of Boot, about 8 miles south east of Gosforth which is just off the A595 Whitehaven to Barrow road.

Distance: 9½ miles (or 4 miles with a short cut).

Map: OS Outdoor Leisure 6: The English Lakes South Western area.

Terrain: The walk, on footpaths and bridleways, involves some long but gradual ascents and descents (the short cut avoids these and includes a short section on a minor road).

Church: St Catherine, the Parish Church of Eskdale.

Car parking: There is parking space between the church and the River Esk, accessed via a narrow byway, opposite the Brook House Inn at Boot. Alternatively, it is possible to park at the Burnmoor Inn in Boot, either as a genuine patron or on the payment of £3.

The Church

The church stands surrounded by its fine graveyard in the Eskdale Valley only a few metres from the River Esk and about 800 metres from the small

Huntsman's memorial in St Catherine's churchyard

hamlet of Boot. It is believed that a church has served the people of the Eskdale valley on this site for over six hundred years. However, the present building is the result of a major rebuilding in 1881. This is the parish church of Eskdale, although there is another church at Eskdale Green, St Bega, dating from 1890.

It is an extremely pleasant and intimate building, consisting, in true dales tradition, of a single chamber, with simple wooden beams and whitewashed walls. There is an absence of the tablets and dedications that characterise so many churches of the 19th century. Leading families and patrons, such as the Reas, Porters, Vicars and Tysons, seem to have been content to assign the stained glass windows to the memory of their loved ones and to ensure that their graves were well-marked.

This was the burial ground for a wide area and the main walk will take you along part of the "corpse road", used to convey the dead from Wasdale to Eskdale for burial until the beginning of the 20th century. The graveyard today is very well cared for and orderly. It is renowned particularly for two interesting huntsmen's gravestones: those of Tommy Dobson and Willy Porter found behind the west wall of the church. There is also a finely worded tablet, by the entrance porch, in memory of Lancelot Salkeld Porter, a founder member of the Lakeland Dialect Society, whose knowledge would have been useful to translate the sign you will find after passing Low Place on the wall!

Among the other features of interest are:

❖ The font, thought to be of 17th-century origin, which includes among its decoration, the wheel, the instrument of St Catherine's martyrdom.

❖ The 16th-century bell on the north window sill. The church guide contains a helpful explanation of its significance and that of the two bells hanging in the bellcote.

❖ The finely carved wooden panelling behind the altar.

❖ The board dated 1798, on the wall beside the south door, giving details of bequests to the poor and the school.

Information available in the church:

❶ *St Catherine's Church Eskdale.*

The Walk

Leave St Catherine's churchyard **(A)**, turn right and then left before the River Esk at a National Trust sign. Follow the clear path to go through a gate and continue along the permitted footpath signposted to Gill Force Bridge. Cross the gated bridge, turn right and walk along a small gully. In a short distance strike off right through the bracken, on one of several paths, to return to the riverbank. Walk downstream and, when you are opposite St Catherine's Church, you will find a gate on your left **(B)**.

Go through the gate and turn right to cross a small beck (you may need to search for an appropriate crossing point following heavy rain). Now follow the track through the trees with the river on your right. Go through a gate, over a footbridge and then through another gate to cross some grazing land. After going through the gate at the end of the field, follow the direction of the public bridleway sign "Forge Bridge 1½ miles; Eskdale Green 2 miles" to cross a track and take a stile next to a metal gate some 20 metres ahead. Follow the public bridleway a short distance to pass through a gate at the edge of the woods. Over to the right you will see the rounded chimneys of Dalegarth Hall.

Now continue ahead on the main track through the woods, ignoring the track entering on the right from Dalegarth Hall, to bear right at the fork a few hundred metres further on. Proceed on the clear track and after going through three gates, the track, now stony, brings you back to the riverbank. Eventually you cross a stile next to a gate to enter meadow land. After taking a further stile next to a gate, follow the clear track for about 300 metres via a gate to reach a corrugated iron barn at Milkingstead on your left(C).

Turn right, cross the gated suspension bridge and continue straight across the field to exit via a gate onto the road opposite the Fisherground campsite **(D)**.

(Those who wish to take advantage of a short cut can turn right at this point and walk back up the road, passing Dalegarth station, to arrive at the junction by the Brook House Inn from where they can return to their car.)

To continue, cross the road and walk down the lane opposite, in the direction of the public footpath sign. Continue on the lane as it bears left to the farmyard, follow the footpath sign into the farmyard and bear diagonally left to go between a barn and a cottage, as indicated by a waymark on the wall.

Go through a gate to join a stone walled track and follow it as it bears right and passes through a series of metal gates, finally exiting via a wooden gate to climb to the Ravenglass and Eskdale railway line.

> *The Ravenglass and Eskdale Railway, popularly known as "L'aal Ratty", was originally designed to carry minerals from the local mines and quarries. It had a somewhat chequered commercial history before being rescued by enthusiasts in 1960 and converted into a major attraction for tourists wishing to enjoy a scenic trip. The 15-inch gauge, steam-hauled train runs through the pleasant scenery between Ravenglass and Dalegarth.*

Cross the line, turn left and after a few metres take the stile next to the metal gate on your right. Bear left and follow the path through the bracken to climb up through the wood and then leave by a steep stone stile. Continue straight ahead across the boggy ground with the wire fence on your left. At the end of the fence, cross straight over a track and continue ascending gradually on the clear path ahead. You pass some rocky outcrops and go through a gateway. The path ascends more steeply through the bracken. However, it soon levels off and then descends to a gate at the corner of a wall. Go through the gate and walk down some 50 metres to meet a stony track. Turn right and follow the track with a wall on your left to pass the attractive dwellings of Low Holme. Continue ahead through the gate and down to meet a narrow metalled lane opposite a sign "Forestry Commission Miterdale"(E).

Turn right and follow the metalled lane, with the sound of the River Mite below, to pass through a gate. Proceed ahead and then bear left towards the public bridleway sign by the riverside. A fine place to stop before the long walk up the valley! Follow the sign "Wasdale Head" and cross the bridge over the river. Stay on the track as it bears right and follow it and eventually go through a metal gate and pass Low Place cottage on your right. Bear right through the farm gates onto the bridleway signposted to Wasdale and continue with the wall on your left. Note the local dialect sign on the wall, "Hod reet fur Eshdel", and remember the memorial to a member of the local dialect

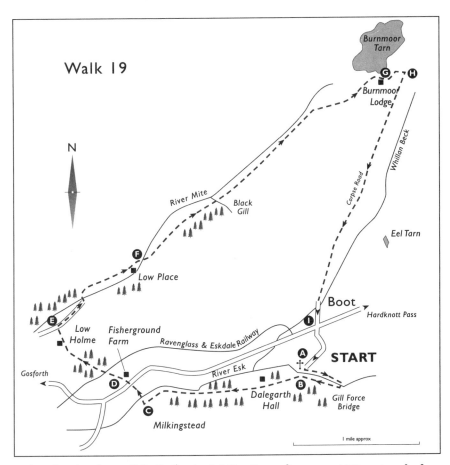

Walk 19

N

Burnmoor Tarn

G -- **H**

Burnmoor Lodge

Corpse Road

Whillan Beck

River Mite

Black Gill

Eel Tarn

F

Low Place

E

Low Holme

Fisherground Farm

Ravenglass & Eskdale Railway

Boot

Hardknott Pass

I

A

START

Gosforth

River Esk

D

Dalegarth Hall

B

Gill Force Bridge

C

Milkingstead

1 mile approx

society by the door of St Catherine's! Continue for some 100 metres before turning right to cross a slightly concealed bridge **(F)**.

Turn left and follow the clear track with the River Mite on your left. The next two miles may seem long, but your route is straight towards the valley head. Generally the path is clear, with the occasional gateway, and you should ignore the temptation to follow tracks off to the left. After a stile next to a gate, a slate sign reassures you that you are on the correct path. Then cross the Black Gill at the most convenient point and continue ahead. After a ladder stile, the valley begins to close in even more. The river varies in strength at times, but it becomes closer at hand as you proceed up the valley. Occasionally the path is very faint, there are a couple of rocky scrambles and the path even disappears shortly before some thick bracken, but just persevere and you will pick it up again a few metres above the riverbank. Eventually you drop down to continue upstream very close to the side of the river. The time to watch carefully is just before you enter the valley head. Look out for some substantial crags which appear on the left and just before you reach these, as the impressive head of the valley basin comes into view, you need to look for a right fork where the faint path climbs through the bracken. (If you go too far you may end up scrambling up the side of the valley or having to retreat to find a path). Follow the path that takes you above the head of the valley. Continue ascending, gradually moving away from the head of the valley, and aiming for the left-hand edge of the hill ahead on your right. Again the way is vague and boggy in parts but suddenly you will be rewarded with a view of the extensive Burnmoor Tarn. Then the next landmark should soon be in view in the form of a solitary tree over to the right of the tarn. Make your way over the rough marshland towards the tree and the outbuilding beside it. Finally as you get closer, Burnmoor Lodge gradually appears to the right of the tree **(G)**.

Sadly the lodge is boarded up, but after passing the front door you may like to read the text on the east gable end, and you may even find something of interest in the little wooden box on the wall! Leave the lodge through the broken wall and follow the broad path, which soon bears left and comes to a crossroads of paths. To the left are Wasdale Head, Great Gable and Scafell Pike, but your route is straight ahead towards the crags and scree of Eskdale Fell. A short way through the gorse and you will meet a track, Burnmoor Tarn Road, popularly known as the "corpse road" **(H)**.

Turn right and follow the old carriageway which was used to bring the dead for burial from Wasdale to St Catherine at Eskdale. Your route back to Boot and St Catherine, Eskdale is now clear. A few cairns confirm you are on the right track, but just keep going straight ahead. The track is quite stony in parts and boggy in others. Eel Tarn appears ahead to the left and Whillan Beck, which runs from Burnmoor Tarn through Boot to the River Esk, gradually gets closer on your left as you descend. Eventually you pass through a gate with a National Trust notice on it and you know that you are half-way down the road! After going through a second gate, ignore the temptation to veer off on a track going left, and instead pass through a gate a few metres ahead and continue in the same direction. You then pass through a few more gates before reaching the metalled road of Boot with the old Eskdale Mill on your left. Shortly after crossing the packhorse bridge over the Whillan Beck, you will find a useful Local District Information Point on a wall opposite the Burnmoor Inn. St Catherine's Church is a little more than 800 metres ahead as you continue down the road to the Brook House Inn to meet the Gosforth-Hardknott Pass road **(I)**.

Cross over and follow the public byway track signposted "St Catherine's Eskdale Parish Church". You pass Felocitas, East View and Kirkhouse on the stony track before reaching the church and the end of the walk.

Walk 20: Gosforth
Celts, chimneys and caravans

Location: St Mary's Church (NY073036) is at the east end of Gosforth. Gosforth is just off the A595, 5 miles north-west of Ravenglass.

Distance: 4½ miles.

Map: OS Outdoor Leisure 6: The English Lakes South Western area.

Terrain: Mostly on the level with a few gentle ascents and mainly on field paths and farm tracks.

Church: St Mary, Gosforth:

Car parking: There is a public car park in the village. Parking is also available on the roads near the church.

The Church

The church is best known for the Gosforth Cross (see below) and the other items in the fine collection of Anglo-Saxon and Anglo-Danish works but the church merits a visit in its own right.

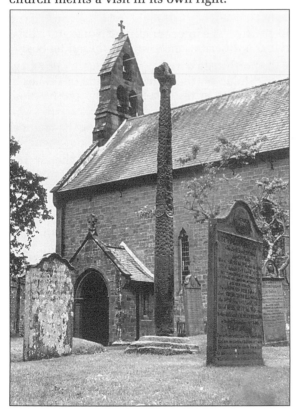

The Christian presence in Gosforth goes back more than 1000 years but the origins of the present building date back to a Norman church built about 1100, on the site of an earlier building. This was largely rebuilt in the 13th and 14th centuries and there have been several restorations and rebuildings over the centuries. Most of what is now seen, a red sandstone building of nave, chancel and bellcote, is from the rebuilding of 1896-9 with elements of Norman and later work still visible. In 1995 an extension was built against the north wall to serve as a meeting room.

Entry to the church is through the porch in the south-west corner.

Gosforth cross and St Mary's Church

Inside, the layout and major furnishings are late Victorian – a long nave with a north aisle, solid pews leading into the chancel with its choir stalls and the high altar. The Victorian influence is continued by the stained glass windows and memorial tablets and plaques. In addition, however, there many other interesting features – both ancient and modern – to investigate. The excellent guidebook provides an easy to follow route through them. It is interesting to note that visitor numbers necessitated the eight reprint of the guide in 2000. There is a feeling of "busyness" here which, nevertheless, does not preclude finding solitude and sanctity in this place.

Among the other features of interest are:

❖ The 19th-century stone font.

❖ The ancient Boundary Stone displayed on the window sill, opposite the porch on the north wall.

❖ Two hogback tombstones at the west end of the north aisle. Known as the "Saint's Tombstone" and the "Warrier's Tombstone", they were retrieved from the Norman foundations during the 1886-9 rebuilding. The "hogback" shapes are covered in carvings – thought to be the work of the man who carved the Gosforth Cross The intermingling of Norse and Christian symbolism in the carvings is described more fully in the guidebook.

❖ The arch at the east end of the north aisle which incorporates ancient fragments including the Fishing Stone, on the right-hand side of the arch, thought to be part of a stone frieze in the chancel of the pre-Norman church.

❖ The two decorated Norman capitals on the pillar supporting the chancel arch.

❖ The Gosforth Cross which is one of four that once stood in the church grounds and which, at 4.2 metres high, is the tallest Viking cross in England. In form it is a tall thin shaft surmounted by a Celtic cross. The slender shaft was carved with its mysterious and intricate scenes around AD940. The survival of the Gosforth Cross ensures that the interlinked Norse and Christian symbolism – dating from before the end of the first millennium – can be appreciated by visitors coming here at the beginning of the third millennium.

Information available in the church:

❶ *A guide to St Mary's Church Gosforth.*

❶ A leaflet, *Short History of St Mary's Church, Gosforth,* Ella Tyson.

The Walk

Leave the church **(A)** and grounds by the lych-gate and cross the road. Turn right, walk past the school and after a few metres turn left at Kirkstile into the narrow lane which runs alongside the school field. Walk to the end of this short lane. At the junction, turn left and walk along the road, passing the Horse and Groom pub on the right. After 800 metres or so, the road crosses

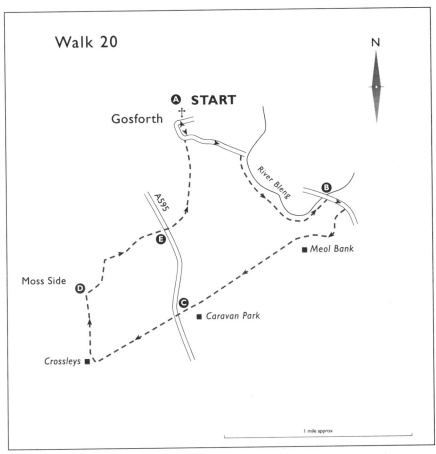

Walk 20

N

O START

Gosforth ✝

River Bleng

A595

B

E

■ Meol Bank

Moss Side

D

C

■ Caravan Park

Crossleys ■

I mile approx

the River Bleng via a hump back bridge. Just before the bridge there is a public footpath sign "Bleng Bridge" on the right. Go through the gate and walk along the path with the river on your left. The path crosses a number of stiles. Ignore the white waymark pointing right and continue until the path reaches a gate leading to a road at Bleng Bridge **(B)**.

Go through the gate, turn right and walk a couple of hundred metres, then turn right onto the farm track indicated by the public footpath sign showing "Meol Bank, Stubshead Lane, Snowder". Where the track divides, turn right and follow the track as it climbs gently to reach Meol Bank Farm. After passing the farm, the track divides again and again you turn right. The track climbs and at its highest point the triangulation pillar on the top of Gallows Hill is visible on the right. Behind, and to the left, there are mountain views and the "gateway to Wasdale" and ahead are glimpses of the Irish Sea and white vapour rising from the towers of the Sellafield complex. Continue on the track as it descends to go past a farm building on your right and the Seven

Acres Caravan Park over to the left. Turn right onto the metalled section of road and walk the short distance to reach the A595 **(C)**.

Cross the road, taking care, turn left and walk to the farm road marked "Public Bridleway" going off to the right. Take this road and continue until a house called Crossleys is in sight. Just before this property, at a children's crossing sign, there is a gate with a yellow waymark on the right. Go through the gate into the field and walk straight ahead up the field with the hedge on your left to reach a ladderstile. Cross the stile into the next field. At this point, Sellafield in all its glory comes into view! This complex might not be the most aesthetically pleasing aspect on this walk but it is one of the most important mainstays of the local economy. However, Sellafield slowly disappears from view as the direction now is to turn half right and walk diagonally over the field aiming for a point near to the left-hand edge of the line of trees on the field boundary and keeping the little rise on your right. At the field edge, cross by the stone stile and, as shown by the yellow waymark, proceed straight across the field to reach a stone stile and a wooden stile. Cross these and continue in the same direction aiming for the corner of a small barn ahead. Carry on in the same direction, now walking with a wire fence on your right. Cross the stile next to the gateway and walk past the barn on your right. Turn right following the line of the wall of the small enclosure, part of Moss Side farm, to arrive at a stile **(D)**.

Cross the stile and proceed over the field following the direction of the waymark keeping the hedge on your left. At the end of the field go over the stile and walk up the field edge with the hedge on your right. After about one hundred metres turn right via the metal gate and walk up the field edge with the hedge on your left. Continue straight ahead with hedge on your left to cross a stile and pass another stile near a gateway. There is a plantation on the right and trees ahead. The path descends to reach a gate leading onto a road, opposite the white railings of Harecroft Hall School **(E)**.

Go through the gate, cross the A595 which can be busy, turn right and in a few metres turn left as indicated by the public footpath sign to Gosforth Village. The path runs alongside the wooded grounds of Harecroft Hall School on the left and a sports field on the right. At the end of the sports field go via a kissing gate into the next field and walk to the end and cross the stream by the footbridge. Cross the field to a gate on the left-hand side. Go through the gate and along the path which runs between fences and hedges and comes out via a gate at Fell View Park, an estate of bungalows and static homes. Walk through the estate and go ahead following the yellow waymark to walk alongside more properties. Continue straight ahead until just after Hillcrest on your right where a yellow waymark directs you up a path past the Mountain Rescue Post to emerge onto a road. Turn left, cross the road, and take the narrow road running alongside the school to arrive back at the church and the end of the walk.

Walk 21: Ulpha and Seathwaite
White Kirk, Wonderful Walker and Wallowbarrow

Location: St John's Church (NY197933) is in Ulpha, which is 4 miles north-west of Broughton-in-Furness. It is on a minor road off the A595, 800 metres west of the A595/A593 junction.

Distance: 9½ miles.

Map: OS Outdoor Leisure 6:The English Lakes South Western area.

Terrain: Mainly on public footpaths over fells with some riverside walking. There are several short, steep ascents and two stony descents.

Churches: St John the Baptist, Ulpha; Seathwaite Church.

Car parking: Parking is available near Ulpha Church.

The Churches
St John the Baptist, Ulpha

The church is situated above the river in the beautiful Duddon Valley. The River Duddon used to be the boundary between Cumberland and Lancashire with the church just squeezing into Cumberland. It is a typical dales chapel – low, single chamber nave and chancel and a bellcote. However, its white rendering finish makes it stand out from other similar, but rough cast chapels. Wordsworth visited here and remembered it as "The Kirk of Ulpha".

Earlier chapels probably existed here but there are no records of their dates nor, indeed, the date of construction of the present chapel. The first

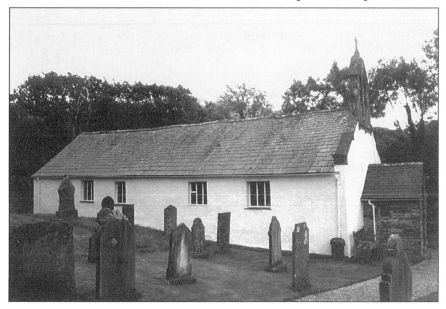

St John the Baptist, Wordsworth's kirk at Ulpha

written mention is in 1577. Ulpha was a chapel-of-ease for the church at Millom and came under Millom's jurisdiction until becoming a separate parish in the 19th century. Several restorations have been carried out, notably in 1882 and 1934 and a wooden porch was replaced with a stone one in 1961. When the ceiling was removed in 1934 fragments of coloured wall drawings from earlier centuries were revealed.

Much of the simplicity associated with the interior of a dales chapel is present at Ulpha – plain walls, exposed roof beams and rows of solid pews leading to a small chancel. Furthermore, there are few memorials and several of the furnishings have been created by church members and local craftsmen. One incumbent, the Revd Chas. Whitaker, who was vicar from 1897 to 1914, made the wooden carved reredos and the brass metalwork panels on the altar.

The church's long association with nearby Ulpha School, which had also received much support from the local Gunson family, came to an end with the closure of the school in 2000. The Gunsons also established the local Almshouses early in the 20th century.

Among the other features of interest are:

❖ The stone font which is pre-Reformation.

❖ The pulpit made by a Broughton-in-Furness joiner Thomas Atkinson. He was 17 when he began the work. Mrs Gunson of Oak Banks provided the funds.

❖ The altar crafted in one piece from a cherry tree in 1882 by a churchwarden Thomas Stephenson.

Information available in the church:

❶ *A Mountain Chapelry in Cumbria*, B.S. Wignall Simpson.

❶ *Duddon Valley History*, J.C. Cooper.

Seathwaite Church

A chapel had existed at Seathwaite for many years before being replaced by the present building in 1874. Although it is not possible to determine the exact age of the older chapel, at the time there were protests against its demolition including efforts made by John Ruskin (see Walk 18, St Andrew, Coniston). Legend has it that a chapel was built here following a petition to one of the Earls of Derby from a funeral party who got stuck here while carrying a body to Kirby-in-Lonsdale.

Originally, Seathwaite was subordinate to Broughton-in-Furness but became a separate parish in 1886. Its longest serving incumbent was the Revd. Robert Walker, (see below), immortalised as "Wonderful Walker" who served for 66 years from 1735 to 1802. A stone used by him for holding sheep for shearing is kept just outside the porch.

The shape of the building – a low, single chamber building with a bellcote and porch – might suggest a typical dales chapel but its slate and stone construction and its interior make it more obviously Victorian. It is pleasantly

Entrance porch, Seathwaite Church

located on the edge of the hamlet of Seathwaite in wooded countryside by the River Duddon.

Inside there are plain walls and exposed roof beams with wooden cladding. Seating in the nave is provided by benches rather than solid pews. The Victorian influence is evident in the incorporation of a chancel arch and choir stalls and by the many stained glass windows and memorials of which there are several to the Revd Walker's descendants. There is a display with a newspaper cutting and other items pertaining to Wonderful Walker near the entrance door. There is a poem about the church by William Wordsworth adjacent to the display. This is a pleasant place to come for a little time of seclusion.

Revd Robert Walker (1709-1802) came from humble beginnings in Seathwaite but gained sufficient education to become a schoolmaster and a Hebrew scholar. He served as a curate/schoolmaster at various places including Loweswater and Buttermere before taking up the incumbency at Seathwaite. Throughout his long working life he supplemented his low stipend by undertaking writing tasks and farming work for people in the parish and he and his wife Anne were virtually self-sufficient. Rising at 4am in winter and 5am in summer to tend his own holding, he was the 18th-century equivalent of a workaholic. His fame spread beyond the Duddon Valley following a reference to him in Wordsworth's writings.

The Walk

Leave Ulpha Church **(A)** by the path to the road and turn left. Walk downhill and continue with the River Derwent on your left for a few hundred metres to a bridge. Cross the bridge and the cattle grid and continue along the road for 100 metres to take the public footpath on the left to "Kiln Bank Cross and Kiln Bank". Walk along the track and follow it up as it winds left to arrive at a house on the left with a gate ahead. Go through the gate and proceed along the forest path to go through another gate. Follow the path to the right and, keeping the wall on your left, carry on to reach an enclosure of Scots pines; this is a former Quaker burial ground known as the "Quaker Sepulchre". Go through a gate and keep on the track as it runs along the Duddon Valley with views to the left of farmland, woods and scattered houses, whilst to the right the country is hilly and more rugged. Carry on for about another mile passing a number of gates before the track descends to Kiln Bank farm. Walk past the farmhouse on your left and climb a short way to exit the farm area by a gate to a bend in a narrow road **(B)**.

Turn right and walk up the road, which becomes steep, the steepest part as it heads towards the summit is Kiln Bank Cross. You will be on this section for 800 metres or so but there are rewarding views to the right over the Duddon Valley. After crossing a cattle grid, walk for 250 metres, then leave the road to take a clear track on the left just after a passing place and head towards the crags ahead. The path winds between the crags and, weather permitting, there is a splendid view to the right to the sea in the distance. Soon the path descends a short way to a definite junction of paths just before a scree-lined hillside **(C)**.

Turn left onto the broad track. From here the route is straightforward all the way to Seathwaite – having joined the "Park Head Road" path. After about 800 metres a stone wall comes in from the left and you walk alongside this for another 800 metres or so before dropping to cross a stream where another path comes in from the right. You continue by bearing left to proceed in the same direction as before for 1200 metres or so. The broad track you are on soon becomes very stony as it descends. The stony track takes you down through a gate marked "Lake District National Park" after which it descends more gently although there are still some tricky stony sections to negotiate before eventually passing three gates in quick succession to emerge onto a road by a sign "Newfield Inn 50 metres". Turn right and walk a short distance to Seathwaite Church **(D)**.

After visiting the church turn right, go through the small gate and cross the road and take the public footpath opposite. After a few metres go through the narrow gap in the wall. Follow the path as it skirts round the trees and crosses a stream by a footbridge. Continue on the path as it makes its way past the disused weir gates Then carry on through an open area, then on a woodland path to descend to cross the River Duddon by a splendid high arched, walled footbridge with gates at both ends **(E)**.

Over the bridge, turn left into the National Trust Wallowbarrow area and

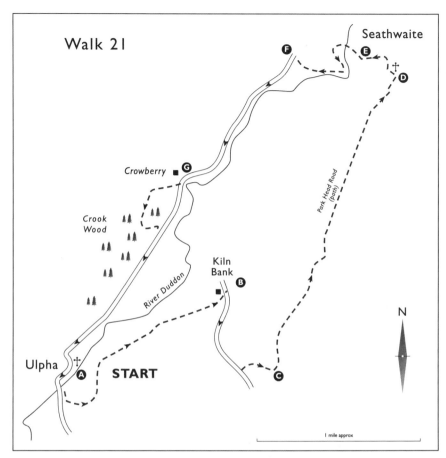

Walk 21

Seathwaite

Crowberry

Crook Wood

Kiln Bank

River Duddon

Park Head Road (path)

Ulpha

START

N

1 mile approx

walk along the river bank, with the river on your left, past stepping stones to come to a kissing gate and a notice giving details about the Ministry of Agriculture, Fisheries and Food conservation walks. Go through the gate and bear left onto the permissive footpath. Follow the waymarked directions through the fields via a series of gates. After about a mile, continue with a wire fence on your left, moving away from the river, to come to a kissing gate and exit to a narrow road **(F)**.

Turn left and walk along the road which runs through wooded areas, with the River Duddon gurgling to your left. After 800 metres or so you reach a junction with a slightly busier road at a bridge. Turn right and walk along this road for about 800 metres and 30 metres after the house called "Crowberry" look for the partially concealed public footpath sign on your right **(G)**.

Climb over the stile and bear slightly left in the direction indicated by the fingerpost to go up the sloping field to find a metal gate about half-way along the wall at the edge of the woods. Enter Crook Wood via the gate, climb straight ahead past a waymark post, and come to a second waymark post. Bear left as indicated to come to another waymark post, then bear right, following the direction shown, to go uphill. Pass a large spoil heap, from the former slate quarry workings, on your left and turn left round this and pass some roofless quarry buildings on your right to meet a stile in the adjacent fence. Cross the stile, walk to a gate, and enter a clearing. Go through this and carry on in the same direction to arrive at further evidence of quarry workings in the shape of more spoil heaps. The actual quarry is not on your route but is some way further on over to the right. Slate quarrying was an extremely important feature of the economy of the Duddon Valley in the nineteenth century. You need to fork left, walk between the spoil heaps, and then bear left to come to a stile near a gate. Cross the stile and follow the steep, stony path down. The stones do not make for easy walking so take care as you descend a short distance to go through another gate, near some ruins. The path is still tricky so take care as you descend to a junction with a road.

Turn right and walk along the road. It is a mile back to Ulpha. As you near the village you can see the Almshouses over to your left. In a short while you enter the village and pass the village shop with its local information board, before arriving back at the church and the end of the walk.

26.5.06

Walk 22: Waberthwaite   Wet.

High level viaduct, high tide flooding and high class purveyor

Location: St John's Church (SD100951) is in the tiny hamlet of Hall Waberthwaite which is on a minor road off the A595, approximately 2 miles south-east of Ravenglass.

Distance: 4 miles (or 3 miles with a short cut).

Map: OS Outdoor Leisure 6: The English Lakes South Western area.

Terrain: Mainly on the level by the Esk estuary and field paths

Church: St John, Waberthwaite.

Car parking: A limited amount of parking is available outside the church.

The Church

The church is in a beautiful spot by a bend in the River Esk sheltered by the Muncaster Fells. Because the river is tidal, it is not unknown for water to be lapping against the churchyard walls in times of high tides. The church is very much at one with the tiny hamlet of Hall Waberthwaite and at first sight seems to be almost a part of the farm complex there. It is a typical dales chapel, a low white building with nave and chancel in one and a bellcote. The windows are of different dates; the west window possibly 14th century, the side windows, possibly 16th or 17th century and the most recent addition the memorial east window from 1931.

There are no written records to establish when the present church was

Ancient cross shaft and St John, Waberthwaite

built but it seems likely that it dates from the 12th century. Interestingly, a deed of 1392 refers to St James of Waberthwaite thus casting doubt on the antiquity of its present dedication to St John the Evangelist. It is thought that there was an earlier church on the site and supporting evidence for this comes from the existence of shafts of old crosses in the churchyard.

Inside the church you see a low ceiling, plain walls with little ornamentation and a tiny sanctuary at the east end; just what you would probably expect to see in a small dales chapel. What sets Waberthwaite apart from many of them is the set of numbered box pews installed in a refurbishment of 1806. These are still used today, with the provision of heaters being a concession to modern times! Most of what you see now dates from the 1806 refurbishment which included putting in a ceiling and a flagged floor. St John's is a place of peace and tranquillity.

Among the other features of interest are:

❖ On the west window ledge, a bell, dated 1882, transferred from St Luke's Chapel which formerly stood in a field now occupied by Waberthwaite School (at the junction of theA595 leading to Waberthwaite village).

❖ The very low solid sandstone font, probably Norman, on the left of the entrance.

❖ The carved oak pulpit, dated 1630.

❖ The two large wooden tablets on the east wall setting out, on the left, the Apostles' Creed and the Lord's Prayer, on the right the Ten Commandments. From 1561 churches were required to display the Ten Commandments. The style of lettering suggests the tablets date from the end of the 16th century.

❖ In the churchyard, standing vertically in its socket stone, part of a cross shaft. The interesting carvings are partially obscured. Research suggests a date between AD850 and AD1000.

Information available in the church:

❸ *St John's Church Waberthwaite.*

❸ *Waberthwaite 2000.*

The Walk

Leave the church **(A)** and grounds by the gate and walk to the public footpath sign about thirty metres ahead on the right. Go onto the path and turn left with the estuary over to your right. There are attractive views over the Waberthwaite Marsh and the Eskmeals Viaduct can be seen in the distance. Continue on the path, part of the Cumbria Coastal Way, which can be very muddy at times owing to tidal flooding. Carry on in the same direction for a few hundred metres as the path enters a lane between two field boundaries with hedges on either side. Proceed along this lane, ignoring the turn off to the left. In a few hundred metres go through a gate, turn right, and walk the

Walk 22

Eskmeals
Viaduct

START

Hall Waberthwaite

Esk Estuary

Newbiggin

Bridge
End

Waberthwaite

N

I mile approx

short distance to cross a footbridge to the left of a ford to emerge onto a road in the hamlet of Newbiggin **(B)**.

The road to the right leads towards the viaduct and is subject to flooding. If you are fortunate, or unfortunate depending on your viewpoint, to be walking after heavy tidal flooding, you might see some spectacular inundations by making a short detour along the road to the right.

To continue on the walk from the footbridge, cross the road to the public footpath sign and go over the stile and along the path between the houses. At the end of this section cross the stile into the field and walk straight ahead with the hedge on your left. At the end of the field go through the kissing gate to the right of a metal gate and continue in the same direction with the hedge now on your right. Go through another kissing gate near a gateway**(C)**.

Continue for about 50 metres to a wide gateway. Pass through the gateway. At this point you leave the Cumbria Coastal Way (which makes for the farm buildings via a footbridge). Go through the gate and walk diagonally left across the field to find a slightly concealed stile about half way along the hedgerow. Cross the double stile and bear right to follow the hedgerow on your right. After a short distance you will see a stream on your right. The path follows the line of the stream going along the fields' boundaries, via a series of stiles, to arrive at a stile to the left of a gate with a track coming in from the right. Carry on with the hedge on your right and go over another stile. Then head straight across the field aiming for a gate. This is a kissing gate and you go through this to emerge onto a road. Turn right and walk the short distance to the small village of Waberthwaite (**D**).

One of the village's attractions is the local shop of Richard Woodall, which combines being a post office and a general dealer but also displays the Royal Warrant as purveyors of traditional Cumberland sausage to the Royal Family.

To continue the walk, retrace your steps the few metres to a public footpath on your right. Take this metalled farm track. Pass a farm gate and a stile and continue down the track. After the track bears to the right, keep walking until the track crosses a little beck. After another 50 metres, and before the entrance to the farm, leave the main track by a clear path on your left. Walk a few metres, cross a stream and go over a stile near a gate. Bear right and make for the telegraph pole at the corner of a field boundary. Then walk up the field a short distance with the hedge on your right. Go over the stile into the next field and walk along the field boundary with the hedge/trees now on your left. At the end of the field go through the opening on your left into the next field and turn right to walk to a stile near a gate. Cross the stile onto a broad lonnen running between hedges. Proceed along the lonnen to exit onto a road (**E**).

(If you wish to take a short cut at this point, you need to turn left and walk back to the church). To continue the walk, turn right and follow the road as it descends to pass Croftwood on your left and then starts to climb. You pass High Woodgate on your right and a few metres beyond this you reach public footpaths coming in from the right and left. Go onto the path on the left via a stile near a gate to enter the woods. Carry on along this delightful woodland path for 400 metres or so to arrive at a stile near a gate. Cross the stile and keep on the path as it descends to a gate. Go through the gate and turn left to walk past the buildings of Bridge End on your right and come to a public footpath sign on your left (**F**).

Enter the field via a stile near a gate and follow the path with a stream on the right to the field corner where there are two adjacent gates. Take the gate on the left and, keeping the hedge/wire fence on your right, cross over the field and carry on towards the left-hand corner of the line of trees ahead on your right. When you reach the corner of the trees bear diagonally left and walk up the slope. When a wood comes into view ahead, walk to the stile, which is about 50 metres from the field boundary fence on the right. Cross the stile into the woods and follow the path, which is indistinct in places, straight ahead for a short distance between the trees to exit the wood via a stile into a field. Bear left and walk along the field edge with trees on your left, ignoring tracks off to the left, until you reach the end of the wood. Bear left round the wood to a kissing gate near a metal gate. Go through the kissing gate then climb up the field keeping the trees on your left to arrive at Cross. Go through the metal gate and follow the waymarks to emerge via a gate onto a road **(G)**.

Turn right and walk down the narrow road to pass the farm buildings of Hall Waberthwaite and arrive back at the church and the end of the walk.

Walk 23: Wasdale Head

End of the line, shooting a line and a logoline

Location: St Olaf's Church (NY188088) is at Wasdale Head about 8 miles from Gosforth which is just off the A595 Whitehaven-Barrow road.

Distance: 4¾ miles.

Map: OS Outdoor Leisure 6: The English Lakes South Western area.

Terrain: The walk is almost entirely on the level, on clear bridleways and grassy footpaths, with a short section of steady climbing and a corresponding descent.

Church: St Olaf, Wasdale Head.

Car parking: There is ample parking on the village green, 200 metres from the church.

The Church

The church lies among fields and is surrounded by yew trees, slightly to the east of the tiny settlement of Wasdale Head and not far from Wast Water with its somewhat intimidating screes on its southern flank. The road seems interminable at times and as Simon Jenkins (*England's Thousand Best Churches*) says: "Half the pleasure (or pain) of Wasdale Head lies in reaching it".

The mountains form an imposing background to the church. St Olaf's lies at the foot of some of the Lake District's most noted mountains including Great Gable, Lingmell and Yewbarrow, which together form the emblem of the Lake District National Park. It is from here that many begin their ascent up Scafell Pike, England's highest peak. It is, therefore, not surprising that this is a church where climbers and fell-walkers are well-remembered. Even before you enter the church you pass a gravestone recalling the death of two young men on Scafell in 1903. Elsewhere in the graveyard, fine slate stones mark the final resting places of others who have lost their lives on these awesome mountains. And inside the church you will find a number of plaques on the windowsills in memory of people who have dearly loved this area.

The church is a low stone building with a tiled roof and, at first glance, not unlike any of the neighbouring barns. Perhaps that is why many walkers go straight past it! They miss a real treat if they do so! While no evidence remains of the precise date of the foundation of the church, there are records which indicate that it has been here for at least 400 years when it first depended on the Priory at St Bees.

It is a tiny church, said to be one of the smallest in England. You certainly have to make sure not to bump your head on the low timber roof beams, some of which are claimed to be from a Viking ship. Whatever the truth of this story there is certainly a strong Viking connection with Wasdale being a Norse name meaning well-watered valley. With this in mind, in 1977 when the parish parochial council decided it was time to seek a name for the church, it was felt appropriate to dedicate the church to the Viking king and saint, Olaf. This was the same year in which the Victorian oil lamps were dis-

St Olaf, Wasdale – a resting place for climbers

creetly converted to electricity, however, little else has changed and this remains a simple dales chapel with very little adornment, intimately related to its environment.

Among the other features of interest are:

❖ The simple wooden cross above the east window.

❖ The dedication in the bottom right-hand corner of the stained glass east window.

❖ The dated and initialled pew door which is now part of the wall covering on the right side of the altar.

❖ The tiny picture of Naples Needle, a climber's favourite on Great Gable, which is in the window in the south wall. The lines from Psalm 121 are very apt.

Information available in the church:

❶ No literature currently in the church. Enquiries should be made at the Barn Door shop, Wasdale Head, for *The Church at Wasdale Head* by Bill Bailey.

The Walk

After visiting the church **(A)**, return to the bridleway leading up from the car park and continue up the stony track. You may find yourself in the company of walkers setting out for Great Gable ahead, Lingmell to the right or

Yewbarrow to the left. You soon arrive at The National Trust's Burnthwaite Farm **(B)**.

Take the path signed to the left, leave the farm by the wooden gate and turn left. Cross the Fogmire Beck for the first time by a footbridge, turn left and walk about 150 metres to a gate. Go through the gate and follow the green track down as it criss-crosses over the beck. Soon the track becomes wider as you are joined by another path descending on your right and as the Fogmire merges with the Mosedale Beck. Continue ahead with the beck on your right to reach the picturesque old packhorse bridge at Row Head **(C)**.

Cross the bridge – however, before you do so you may wish to go a few metres further and take the stile next to a gate into Wasdale Head itself, to seek refreshment at the Wasdale Head Hotel and visit the well-stocked mountaineers' shop.

> *The Wasdale Head Hotel boasts Ritson's Bar, the home of the world's biggest liar. Will Ritson who was born in the hotel in 1808 was an extremely well-known local personality, a friend to all, even to Wordsworth. This larger than life character was renowned for his witty and exaggerated story telling which on one occasion earned him the accolade of the "biggest liar in the world". A traditional annual story-telling competition still goes on today at nearby Stanton Bridge.*

After crossing the packhorse bridge, turn left and follow the beck downstream. Go through a gate and continue in the same direction until you exit onto the road through a kissing gate. Turn left and cross Down in the Dale Bridge **(D)**.

Continue along the metalled road for a few hundred metres to reach two signs on the right indicating the footpath to Scafell Massif and the bridleway to Eskdale/Miterdale **(E)**. (At this point if you prefer a shorter walk simply continue up the road to arrive back at the car park).

Take the stile next to the gate in the direction "Scafell Massif (via Hollow Stone)" and follow the marker posts straight across the field to pass between some bushes and reach a footbridge over Lingmell Beck **(F)**.

Once over the bridge and through a kissing gate on the right, continue along the clear path as it gently climbs through the bracken. You may like to stop at the next kissing gate to take a breath, to admire Wast Water as it comes more into view and to look back at St Olaf's church, just discernible among the yew trees. The path now becomes steeper and stonier, but the views get better and on a clear day the Irish Sea comes into view on the horizon. Keep straight ahead on the main track until eventually you reach the tumbling waters of Lingmell Gill and a kissing gate through which a stony path descends from Scafell Pike **(G)**.

Don't go through the kissing gate but instead turn right to join the path and follow the beck as it races downstream. Make your way carefully down the stony path to pass through a kissing gate. Follow the line of the fence on your left for about 75 metres and descend to go through a gate and cross a footbridge. Turn right and continue down the other side of the beck to reach a wooden bridge taking you back over the Lingmell Gill **(H)**.

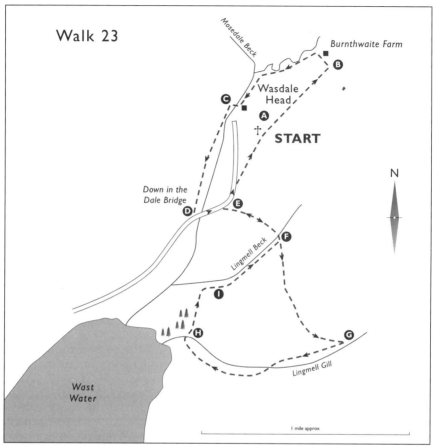

Don't cross the cattle grid ahead, but instead turn right to walk along the side of a wood. Go through a kissing gate on the left and then bear right to pass a campsite on your left. After a waymarked stile next to a gate walk straight ahead for a short distance and then bear right along the bank of the Lingmell Beck (not the Gill this time) towards a waymark post **(I)**.

Continue up the side of the beck, along a ridge of stones. A white waymark indicates the way ahead through the trees and the bracken. Proceed with a stone wall on your right and eventually climb through the broken wall to continue with the wall now on your left and a fence on your right. Take the stile at the footbridge, cross the bridge and go straight ahead across the field to retrace your steps and reach a stile next to a gate **(E)**.

Cross the stile onto the metalled road. Turn right and walk a short distance up the road, back to the car park, the church and the end of the walk.

Walk 24: Cartmel
Canons, carp and a coastal way

Location: Cartmel Priory (SD 380788) is located in Cartmel, which is 1½ miles north west of Grange-over-Sands. It can be approached from the A590 about 2 miles south-east of Newby Bridge.

Distance: Walk 24(a), Cartmel and Bigland Tarn: 8 miles; Walk 24(b), Cartmel only: 6½ miles.

Map: OS Outdoor Leisure 7: The English Lakes South Eastern area.

Terrain: Walk 24(a) is on public footpaths, forest tracks and quiet country lanes with a short section on a slightly busier road. There is some uphill walking involving gradual ascents. Walk 24(b) omits the short section on the slightly busier road.

Church: The Priory Church of St Mary and St Michael (Cartmel Priory).

Car parking: There are parking bays on the roads near the church and a village car park a few hundred metres down the main street.

The Church

The Priory Church of St Mary and St Michael is in the centre of the attractive village of Cartmel. The church's guidebook says that the Priory "dominates the little village of Cartmel" and in the sense that it is the village's most conspicuous feature, that is fair comment. Yet so well are the Priory and the surrounding buildings integrated that there is an overall feeling of appropriate togetherness.

Little is known of the ecclesiastical history of Cartmel before the building of the Priory, but it is likely that there was a church in or near Cartmel before the Norman Conquest. About 1188 the Priory was founded by William Marshall, later Earl of Pembroke, for the order of Augustinian Black Canons. From then until the Reformation, God was worshipped and travellers were welcomed by the monks of Cartmel. The Priory also served as a parish church and, for that reason, the church itself was not destroyed during the Dissolution of the Monasteries. However, apart from the gatehouse, the other monastic buildings did not survive. The Priory continues to serve as the parish church and nowadays provides a welcome for the many tourists who visit it.

During the eighty years after the Dissolution some damage did occur and major restoration work, mainly to the roofs and ceilings was carried out between 1618 and 1633 by George Preston of Holker Hall. What you see today is the Norman church as restored by Preston with some early Victorian restoration including the raised sanctuary floor. Of particular interest is the diagonally positioned bell tower, which is unique in Britain. The importance of Cartmel Priory is underlined by Nikolaus Pevsner *(The Buildings of England: North Lancashire),* "So we have here a complete priory church ... the church can still give us an unparalleled impression of the relation of scale between such a building and the little town at its feet".

The interior of the building is no less rewarding than the outside. One's eyes are drawn irresistibly to the truly magnificent Great East Window with

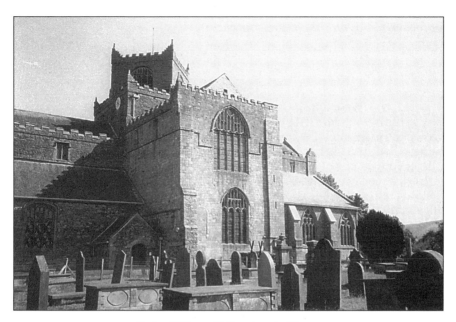

Cartmel Priory with its unique bell tower

its arches and plain glass with stained glass insets, but there is much else to be seen here.

Among the other features of interest are:

❖ The Cromwell door at the south-west corner of the nave; notice the holes said to have been caused by shot from parishioners who fired at Roundhead soldiers who were stabling their horses in the nave.

❖ The modern sculpture *They fled by Night* by Josefina de Vasconcellos (see also Walk 29, St Mary the Virgin, Ambleside), near to the Cromwell door.

❖ The ancient parish chest, formerly containing the church records, by the entrance.

❖ The brass chandelier, given to the church in 1734.

❖ The "bread cupboard", provided under the terms of a legacy, near the north door where two loaves of bread are always available for the poor of the parish (the loaves are changed every Saturday!).

❖ In front of the chancel, the oak screen with its intricate carving from around 1620.

❖ The misericords in the chancel furnishings.

❖ The original lancet window in the north transept.

Information available in the church:

❶ There is a good selection of literature including *The Priory Church of St Mary and St Michael*, Revd Alan Baker (Revised 1996).

The Walks

Walk 24(a), Cartmel and Bigland Tarn: 8 miles

Leave the churchyard **(A)** by the gate at the west end and walk straight ahead down the main street. Where the road divides bear left and carry on past the village hall into the car park. After 50 metres turn right at the notice board, displaying details of access to Cartmel Park, and walk across the grass and cross the race course via a small gate in the railings to arrive at a kissing gate leading into a wood. Go through the gate and onto the path as it goes uphill. The main path winds a little and is crossed by other tracks but is easy to follow. It comes out of the wood near a stone wall. Go through the narrow gap in the wall and proceed along the path with the field boundary on your right to emerge, via another narrow gap, onto a minor road **(B)**.

Turn right and walk along the road. Where the road bends to the right, keep walking to the left past the entrance to Well Knowe farmhouse, Well Knowe Barn and Well Knowe House. Carry on this track as it begins to run between field boundaries. Keep on the track past various outbuildings at a pig farm and at the next junction follow the waymark sign to go a short distance to a waymarked gate. Go through the gate and carry on in the same direction to emerge at a house and outbuildings. Pass in front of the house and turn sharp left between the outbuildings to a waymarked gate **(C)**.

Go through the gate and, bearing slightly right, follow the path as it climbs between the rocky outcrops before descending right to a metal gate. Go through this gate and follow the path as it passes over a little beck. Walk towards a stone stile near palings in the field corner ahead. Cross the stile and proceed straight across the field to another stile. Go over this stile and walk towards the house that is ahead to the left, at the end of the field. Go through the waymarked gate and around Wall Nook farm. Pass the farm and buildings and bear left to cross a cattle grid. Follow the track for a few hundred metres to a second cattle grid and arrive at a minor road **(D)**.

Now turn left and go up the road, which becomes quite steep as it bends past Over Ridge. Just beyond the house take the second track on the right and continue climbing to reach a waymarked gate. Go through the gate and continue on the path to an area of old barns and a caravan. Pass through this area via waymarked gates and continue in the same direction. Look out for a waymark on a rock and bearing to the left of the rock walk ahead aiming for the corner of the forest ahead of you. Go through the gate into Great Allotment Forest. At this point, looking back over the direction you have come from, there are views towards Morecambe Bay. Walk straight ahead with the wall on your right and follow the forest path to arrive eventually at a clearing with a little tarn. Carry on the path as it bears to the right and emerges via a gate onto a minor road **(E)**.

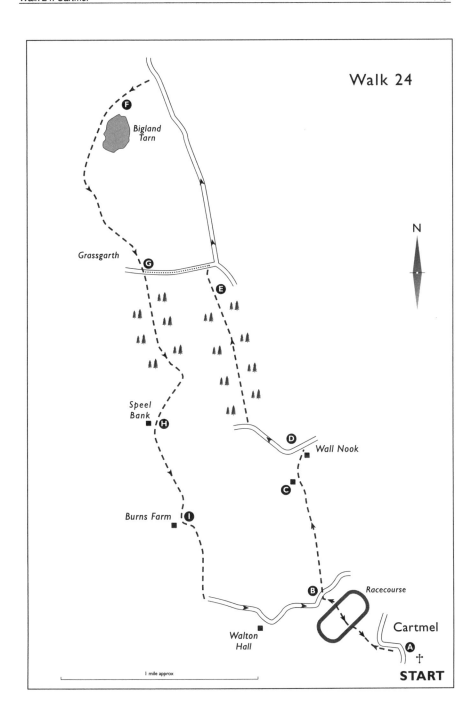

Walk 24

N

Bigland Tarn

Grassgarth

Speel Bank

Burns Farm

Wall Nook

Walton Hall

Racecourse

Cartmel

START

1 mile approx

Turn right and walk the short distance to a road junction. Turn left and go uphill on this busier road for about 1200 metres. It becomes quite steep before you come to the entrance of Bigland Hall Estate on the left. Turn left onto the public footpath and walk along the wide carriageway to come to Bigland Tarn. This is a beautiful spot, quite secluded and home to water lilies, large carp and sleepy anglers. It's about the half-way point on the walk and possibly a suitable place for a picnic stop **(F)**.

Leave the carriageway at the anglers' noticeboard and take the green path as it bears round the tarn, which is on your left. After going through a kissing gate, join the Cumbria Coastal Way. Follow the clear track as it climbs away from the tarn and passes through a waymarked gate. After leaving the tarn the path comes to the open area of Bigland Heights with splendid views of the Leven Viaduct which carries the Carlisle to Settle railway. Continue on the path to reach High Stribers Wood. Go into the wood via a gate and carry on the woodland path to exit through a gate, then bear left to walk towards a house ahead. Follow the path as it passes Grassgarth, crosses a beck and emerges via a kissing gate onto a minor road **(G)**.

Cross the road and go into the fields via the metal gate. You are still on the Cumbria Coastal Way and for the next mile or so you will see the Cumbria Coastal Way (or CCW) waymarks. Walk uphill and follow the waymarks to arrive, via two gates, at a stone stile over a wall. Go over the stile and walk straight ahead, ignoring paths going off to the right and left, to pick up the waymarks and follow these over the open ground with craggy outcrops. Soon after these a wood comes into view ahead. Before reaching the wood look out for a waymark which directs you to the left, towards the middle of the wood. Enter the woods via a gate and keep to the path as it goes between the trees and then runs alongside the boundary wall, on your right, for a short distance, to exit via a gate into an open area. Walk ahead for about 75 metres and bear right and descend to follow the wall on your right. Cross the ladder stile to join a metalled road, turn right and walk to Speel Bank farm **(H)**.

Go through the farmyard and bear right along a walled track for a short distance. If you are lucky you might see some deer over to your right. Go through a metal gate and turn left almost immediately through a second gate by a fingerpost. Walk straight ahead with a wall on your left for a short way and continue over the field to go though a gate. Proceed ahead and then follow a waymark sign to cross to the other side of the field boundary. Continue ahead with a mixture of hedge and wall now on your left. Go through a gate and turn right to follow the CCW sign. Cross diagonally to go through another gate and follow the clear green track with the wire fence on your right. Continue towards Burns Farm, visible ahead on the right. Go through another gate to arrive at a junction of paths. Turn right and continue along the Cumbria Coastal Way to a waymarked gate at Burns Farm. Go through the gate and turn left past the farm buildings to arrive at a minor road going off to the left **(I)**.

Walk along the narrow metalled road past the caravans on your right and continue as the road bears to the right. Carry on past the road entrance to Howbarrow on the right and continue on this pleasant country lane for 800 metres or so to pass Walton Hall farm. Proceed for 500 metres or so until you reach the public footpath sign (slightly concealed) to Cartmel on your right. You have now come back to point **(B)** from where you can retrace your steps to Cartmel, the church and the end of the walk.

Walk 24(b), Cartmel only: 6½ miles

Follow the main walk as far as the end of Great Allotment Forest **(E)**, but instead of turning right on the minor road, turn left and walk along the road for about 800 metres until you reach Grassgarth on your right. Then follow the directions from **(G)**.

Walk 25: Cartmel Fell
Window, woods and Windermere

Location: St Anthony's Church (SD 417881) is at Cartmel Fell, 7 miles from
Bowness on Windermere, on a minor road off the A592 between Bowness and
Newby Bridge. Alternatively it can be approached from Newby Bridge by leaving the
A592 on the Fell Foot Brow road.

Distance: Walk 25 (a), Cartmel Fell including Staveley-in-Cartmel: 8 miles; Walk
25(b), Cartmel Fell only: 4 miles.

Map: OS Outdoor Leisure 7: The English Lakes South Eastern area.

Terrain: The walks are along footpaths, bridleways and very pleasant forest paths
and tracks. Some of the tracks can be quite boggy in parts. Walk 25(a) contains a
short section up a steep minor road. Walk 25(b) omits the forest section and is
mainly on the level.

Church: St Anthony of Egypt, Cartmel Fell.

Car parking: There is parking beside the church.

The Church
St Anthony of Egypt, Cartmel Fell

The church lies almost hidden amid the scattered farms and houses that
make up Cartmel Fell. However, it is well signposted and well worth making
the effort to find. It nestles in a hollow beyond the lych-gate; a rather unpre-
possessing building of mixed stone with a slate roof and a variety of window
shapes. The beauty, however, lies within.

The church dates from the early 1500s and it is the only parish church in
Cumbria to be dedicated to St Anthony of Egypt, patron saint, among other
things, of charcoal burners, appropriate to the woodland activities of the
vicinity. It was built as a chapel-of-ease for the local hill farmers and their
families, to ease them from the long trek to Cartmel Priory.

The interior is surprisingly spacious and simple. Above, the eye is
attracted by the solid timber beams. However, the main thrust is forward and
slightly downwards towards the wooden box pews and the triple-decker
pulpit. The box pews were the privileged seats of the owners of the three
halls found in the locality. "Cowmire", the boxed pew on the north side,
dates from the 16th century when it was the property of the Briggs. It once
doubled as a schoolroom, and the squares cut into the benches are objects of
curiosity. Next to it is the "Thorphinsty pew" a much smaller pew box bearing the date 1696. The two holes in the bench seat, made from an old door,
have given rise to the name "keyhole seat". On the south side is
"Burblethwaite" (rebuilt in 1811) which belonged to the Knipe family, who
together with the Briggs were responsible for the erection of the church in
the first place.

The triple-decker pulpit bears the date 1698 and the vicar still climbs and
preaches from the top tier! An interesting picture on the side of the pulpit
explains the work of the clerk who occupied the lower stall.

St Anthony of Egypt, Cartmel Fell

Among the other features of interest are:

❖ The attractive baptistry created in the base of the bell tower.

❖ The wall tablet to the Poole family on the north wall behind the small box pew. A sad story indeed.

❖ The east window. This is thought to contain pieces of 15th-century glass rescued from Cartmel Priory (see Walk 24) and subsequently re-assembled. In the left-hand light it shows St Anthony, the patron saint of swineherds (as well as of charcoal burners and hermits!), with a boar at the bottom of his staff. The right-hand light is believed to depict St Leonard, like St Anthony, a member of the Augustinian Order to which Cartmel Priory belonged. The three central lights are said to depict the sacraments, although some uncertainty exists as to whether all seven sacraments are still intact. It is apparently based on a 15th-century Dutch painting, a reproduction of which hangs on the side of the nearby box pew.

Information available in the church:

❶ A leaflet, *Saint Anthony's Cartmel Fell.*

The Walks

Walk 25(a), Cartmel Fell including Staveley-in-Cartmel: 8 miles

After visiting the church **(A)**, leave by the lych-gate, pass the old school (1872-1971), and after about 20 metres take the public footpath on your right which soon leads to a quiet lane. Turn right and walk up the lane to the junction with a minor road **(B)**. Cross the road and take the ladder stile. Ahead to the right on the hilltop you may see a cairn. This in fact is a well-constructed monument known locally as "Ravensbarrow Old Man". Continue in the direction of the fingerpost up the grassy path and cross the stone stile. Proceed straight ahead, ignoring paths off to the left and right, and cross the gated ladder stile into the plantation. Walk ahead and leave the plantation by a gated hole in the wall. Follow the clear path as it passes through the bracken to join a stony path. Bear right along the path and through a gate. Continue ahead for about 150 metres between two stone walls and turn left at a waymark sign. Continue along the well-defined track to a metal gate **(C)**.

Go through the gate, turn right and walk up the metalled lane to pass Foxfield farm and the adjacent dwellings. The surface of the lane changes as you climb to go through a gate. About 50 metres after the gate leave the main track and take the public footpath signed to the left **(D)**.

Continue up the faint path to follow the line of the wall on your left. The path winds up beyond the craggy outcrops to meet the wall. At its convergence with another wall, take the waymarked stile into the plantation. Follow the clear path round the edge of the dense forest. After about 400 metres, on entering a small clearing, the path divides at a waymark post on your left which may be partially hidden. Bear right and continue along the main path, taking you more fully into the forest. Just before a waymark post, a path forks off to the left to Simpson Ground Reservoir and you may wish to stroll 100 metres or so to enjoy a break there, otherwise just keep going in the direction of the waymark sign. Keep to the clear path although you may need to circumvent some boggy sections. Eventually, after passing a waymark post, where another track joins from the right, you enter a clearing and meet a forest road. Continue straight ahead and walk down the forest road After a while you find that the forest has been subject to a major clearance operation on your right. When the south end of Windermere comes into view, you need to look carefully to locate a small waymark post on your right **(E)**.

Turn right and leave the forest road in the direction of the waymark to pass through the clearance area. Go through the gate in the fence, ignoring a waymark sign off to the right after about 20 metres, and follow the path straight ahead to a gate in the stone wall. Go through the gate and make your way down to cross the field on a faint path that zig-zags towards the stone wall at the bottom. Just before the wall, bear left along a clear path to a waymarked gate. Go through the gate and continue straight ahead on the track between the trees, passing the houses to meet a minor road with a telephone box on the right **(F)**.

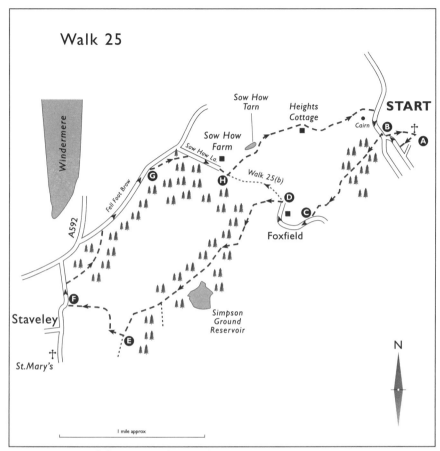

Walk 25

You may like to make a detour to the church of St Mary at Staveley-in-Cartmel some 400 metres straight down the road to the left, just beyond the old school (1875), now the church hall. The present church is mainly a result of the restoration that took place at the end of the 19th century, although there has been a church here since 1618. Inside the lych-gate are inscribed the names of those from the parish who served and died in the two World Wars and the variety of the regiments represented makes interesting reading. The clock tower is attractive and through the windows you can make out the fine timber roof. While the church is generally closed, it stands within a well cared for graveyard and there is nice seat conveniently placed by the main door where a weary walker could rest for a while!

To continue, turn right past the telephone box and walk up the road to pass The School House noting the interesting plaque on the wall. Leave the road at the public footpath sign to Fell Foot on the right and cross the gravel yard of Lyne Riggs to go through the waymarked gate on the right. Follow the path and soon pass through a gate and then almost immediately turn left to cross a waymarked stile into the wood. A clear path now takes you just beyond a waymark post to a stone stile. Cross the stile, bear right for a few metres before bearing left at a low waymark post which may be concealed by the bracken. Follow the clear path as it winds through the wood keeping to the left of the crags to exit through a gap in the wall onto Fell Foot Brow, a minor road. Turn right. Now you have a very steady pull up for about 800 metres, but beware of the traffic which tends to descend rather too quickly on occasions. You may like to take the opportunity to stop from time to time to admire more views of Windermere. Ahead to the left is Gummer's How, a popular climb. Leave the road on the right to go into the Forestry Commission Gummer's How car park and picnic area **(G)**.

Leave the car park by the broad track on the left. Almost immediately the path divides, ignore the permissive path signposted off to the left, and carry straight on along a well-trodden path which leads towards the top of the plantation and through the edge of the forest to emerge onto another minor road, Sow How Lane, through a gap in the wall. (Although this is not a right of way, it enjoys the benefit of the Forestry Commission's open public access policy. It could, however, be closed for clearance and other work, in which case it would be necessary to continue up the road until you reached the first turning on the right onto Sow How Lane). Turn right and follow Sow How Lane to the farm. Go straight ahead through the farmyard and about 100 metres after the metal gate turn left at the public bridleway sign **(H)**.

Continue along the clear track and through the gate. Sow How Tarn becomes visible on your left as the path skirts round some trees. Follow the waymark signs which lead you right through a broken wall and over meadow land to a waymarked gate through which you enter the wood. Follow the track in the direction of the waymarks to go through a wooden gate. Continue ahead until the track bends round to the right to reach Heights Cottage, undergoing restoration at the time of writing. Keep on the grassy path with the stone wall on your left and a small plantation on your right. Go through the gate and continue on the clear path for a further 200 metres or so to take the path to the left where the path divides. Follow the green path, climbing slightly to pass some craggy outcrops on your left, and bear right with the path as it levels out. Now you will see the track more clearly as it descends and becomes more rutted. This track leads down through a wooden gate and then a metal gate onto a minor road. Turn right and climb up the metalled lane to arrive back at a junction **(B)**.

Fork left at the sign for the church and then immediately take the public footpath on the left to St Anthony's Church. The path takes you through a narrow gap in the wall to the church and the end of the walk.

Walk 25(b), Cartmel Fell only: 4 miles

Follow Walk 25(a) to just beyond Foxfield **(D)**. However, do not bear left at the public footpath sign. Instead continue straight along the stony farm track and through two gates eventually to arrive at a public bridleway sign just before Sow How Farm. Turn right along the bridleway and proceed as from **(H)** above.

Walk 26: Colton and Tottlebank
Ringers, Russland and Reformation rule-breakers

Location: Holy Trinity Church (SD 318861) is on a minor road out of Colton. Colton is 4 miles north of Ulverston and can be approached from a minor road from the A5092 at Penny Bridge near the junction of the A5092 and the A590.

Distance: 6 miles.

Map: OS Outdoor Leisure 7: The English Lakes South Eastern area.

Terrain: Mostly on public footpaths with some walking on minor roads. There are several short but quite steep ascents.

Churches: Holy Trinity, Colton; Tottlebank Baptist Church.

Car parking: There is car parking outside the church grounds.

The Churches
Holy Trinity, Colton

Holy Trinity Church is in an attractive position at the top of a steep rise above the small hamlet of Colton and with extensive views over gentle rolling countryside. Externally the building consists of a square embattled west tower, a single chamber nave and chancel, a wide porch and a north transept. From the outside it is a sturdy, no-nonsense church set in a large, well-kept graveyard. Over the road is the former school which dates from 1745.

In pre-Reformation times, the district around Colton belonged to Furness

Sturdy tower at Holy Trinity, Colton

Abbey and this and other outlying areas were served by monks from the Abbey operating from granges. It is not possible to determine the exact date when a chapel was built at Colton itself but there are traces of 15th-century work in the present building and it is known that such a chapel existed by 1530. In 1578 the then existing chapel was enlarged and consecrated as a parish church.

Since that time there has been a series of rebuilding and restoration works, the last major restoration being carried out in 1890. A few years later in 1897 an ancient bell, thought to be 14th century, was rediscovered after being neglected in the belfry for centuries. It is of great interest to visiting campanologists.

On entering the church, looking east to the step leading to the chancel there is a feeling of length here-and, indeed, this place is bigger than a typical dales chapel. The side windows which are square-headed and of different shapes and sizes date from the 16th century. However, the form and furnishings of the interior are essentially the result of the 1890 restoration. The walls are heavily adorned with a variety of memorials and other plaques. Internally, this is a church with a Victorian appearance. There is a peaceful atmosphere here, a place for solitude.

Among the other features of interest are:

❖ The 15th-century octagonal stone font. It was rediscovered in 1890 having been used for two centuries as the base of a later font.

❖ The two war memorials: for 1914-18 a stained glass window in the south wall; for 1939-45 a board with a copper cross on the west wall.

❖ The stone reredos from 1890, a gift from Mrs Cuthbertson who also gave the east window.

❖ In the churchyard, visible from the south west door, a sundial erected in 1998 to replace one stolen in 1997.

Information available in the church:

❶ *Holy Trinity Church, Colton, notes on its history and environs*, Enid Barwell. This also contains notes on Tottlebank Baptist Church.

Tottlebank Baptist Church

Tottlebank Baptist Church is a single-storey plain rectangular building. Although not generally open, apart from service times, much of the interior can be viewed through the plain glass windows. Inside are fine dark oak boxed pews and other furnishings. Behind the church is the graveyard. The church was built in 1699 but the beginnings of a worshipping community here dates back to 1669.

At that time, following the Restoration of Charles II and the Church of England as the exclusive Established Church, life was not easy for those not conforming to the latter's practices. Nevertheless, a group of seven men met at Tottlebank and set up a "Church of Christ". They met in various houses, mostly in secret, until the Toleration Act of 1689. Funds were obtained and the church was built in 1699. In the early years of the 18th century the "Church of Christ" gradually came to adopt specifically Baptist practices.

During the last quarter of the 20th century membership declined and the church closed in 1980. However, and in a repetition of what had happened 300 years earlier, meetings in private houses began again in 1986 and the church itself was reopened in 1989. A new pastor was appointed, perhaps appropriately, in 1999 – ready to carry Tottlebank Baptist Church into the new millennium.

The Walk

Leave the church **(A)** and grounds by the gate leading to the minor road. Turn right to walk to a metal gate. Pass through the gate and follow the track upwards in the direction of the "byway" waymark sign. The track climbs steeply for a short way then descends towards the trees on your left. Make your way down to pass through a gate into woods. There is a notice here indicating that the woods are in the care of The Woodland Trust. Walk along the pleasant woodland track to emerge via a gap near a gate onto a minor road **(B)**.

Turn right and proceed for a few hundred metres down the narrow road with trees on both sides. Keep on this road passing a road off to the left to Hay Bridge and take the next road off to the left. Walk up this road passing the Old School House (indicated by a low sign on the ground) on your right. Follow the road past other properties and carry on, ignoring any roads and tracks going off, until you reach a "single track" sign. Continue on, past the sign, to come to a narrow road going off to the left; about twenty metres down this road is a sign "Black Beck Farm". Take this road and follow it past the farm and the caravan site seen through the trees on the right and then through an area of woodland. In 800 metres or so you come to a cattle grid. Just before this look for the public footpath sign on your right **(C)**.

Go onto the path and follow it through the woods for a few hundred metres and then look out for a yellow waymark indicating a path on the left. Take this path for 800 metres or so as it meanders through the woods, going over a wooden boarded section over a boggy area with a waymark showing the direction. The path emerges from the woods at Fish House Bridge to come to a signposted crossing of footpaths **(D)**.

Take the path to "The Causeway" on the right walking along the canal-like section of the Russland Pool that is on your right. To the left in an area known as The Crams are fields with tree covered hills beyond. Continue on the path on the top of the embankment with the river on your right passing a number of stiles until you emerge via a waymarked stile onto a road. **(E)**.

At this point you are about 800 metres from the busy A590 which crosses the river further down. You need, now, to turn right to cross the bridge and then immediately turn left (there is no footpath sign) to walk along the path with the river now on your left. You soon pass a kissing gate near another gate. Keep on the clear track for a few hundred metres to go through a metal kissing gate. About 120 metres further on, immediately after crossing a small beck, turn right in the direction of the waymark and walk towards a gap at the left-hand edge of the hedge ahead. Go onto the lonnen as indicated by the waymark and carry on between stone walls to arrive at two gates leading onto a road, opposite a house. Turn left and walk up the road for about two hundred metres to a public footpath sign on your left. Take the path into the woods. In a short while you pass a path close to a small sewage plant on your right. Carry on in the same direction and, at a crossing of paths, go straight ahead at the waymark post. Ignore paths to the left and right and descend to cross a little stream (if it is high you can cross a few metres upstream). Continue on the path ahead as it climbs a short way before descending gradually to go through a gap in the wall to three waymarks **(F)**.

Walk straight ahead, up the slope and cross the field to pass a waymarked stile. Carry on straight across the next field to a waymarked ladder stile into the woods ahead. Bear left along the narrow path and after about 50 metres keep left at a fork in the path before descending through the woods to emerge via a gap stile onto a road. Turn right and walk the short distance to a junction which is signposted for "Snows and Colton". Go on the road to the left There is quite a steep pull up here but shortly after passing Mill Gate there are rewarding views over the River Leven to the estuary. Follow the road as it descends to pass Snows and after a further 200 metres arrives at a junction with the interesting modern property of Little Mill on the corner. Turn left and walk down the narrow road the short distance to Little Mill Bridge over the stream **(G)**.

Immediately after the bridge take the public footpath on the right and walk uphill through the woods to arrive at a rickety metal gate. Go through this gate and head straight across the field to reach a gap in the hedge – you might not recognise the gap until you almost reach it because it is concealed by overlapping hedges. Go through the gap and, bearing right, walk around the field boundary with the hedge on your right until you arrive at a wooden gate about 100 metres from the top of the field. Go through the gate and then bear diagonally left to exit via another gate onto a road near some properties. Turn right and walk past the Old Parsonage to Tottlebank Baptist Church **(H)**.

Having viewed the church through the plain glass windows, go through the gate between the church and churchyard and walk across the field to a kissing gate. Go through the gate and turn right. Walk ahead across the field bearing slightly right to come to a kissing gate. Go through the kissing gate and follow the line of the wall on your left. In a short while you pass through a gap in the fence. As you descend you bear round a rocky outcrop on your right and a hedge now appears on your left. Continue on to pass between the rocky outcrops and make for a line of rocks with a telegraph pole behind them. Follow the line of rocks down the field aiming for the left-hand corner of the woods ahead. Exit onto a minor road via a gate. Turn right, cross Hell Pot Bridge and walk uphill to a road junction. Turn left and walk along this

Walk 26

START
Colton

Ridding Side
Farm

The Old
School
House

Black Beck
Farm

River Russland Pool

Fish House
Bridge

The Crams

Tottlebank

N

1 mile approx

road for about 800 metres passing Ridding Side Farm on your left. After another 200 metres you come to a public footpath sign on the right(I).

Take the public footpath and follow it as it climbs aiming to find a gap in a stone wall in the top right-hand corner of the field. However, there are several possible paths and some boggy areas to be negotiated before you come to the stone wall. Follow the grassy path upwards bearing right to pass under two separate sets of telegraph wires. Continue climbing to follow a third set of wires for about 20 metres before bearing right to pass beneath these. Carry on to reach a steep bankside of heather. Bear left and continue upwards and soon pass a large pond on your left before arriving at the stone wall. Go through the narrow gap in the wall. Carry on in the same direction. Shortly, Colton Church comes into view. When you reach the churchyard wall make for the right-hand corner and follow the wall, with the church on your left, to arrive at a stile. Cross the stile and turn left to return to the church and the end of the walk.

Walk 27: Grasmere
Laureate, lakes and Loughrigg

Location: St Oswald's Church (NY 337074) is in Grasmere, which is just off the A591 between Keswick and Ambleside.

Distance: Walk 27(a), Grasmere and Alcock Tarn: 6 miles; Walk 27(b), Grasmere only: 4 miles.

Map: OS Outdoor Leisure 7: The English Lakes South Eastern area.

Terrain: Both walks are largely on footpaths. There is a long and at times steep climb in Walk 27(a) while Walk 27(b) is generally more on the level.

Churches: St Oswald, Grasmere; Grasmere Methodist Church; Our Lady of the Wayside RC Church, Grasmere.

Car parking: There is a limited amount of parking with an honesty box in St Oswald's Church car park on the minor road opposite the church. There are two pay and display car parks within easy reach.

The Churches
St Oswald, Grasmere

This must be one of the most visited churches in the Lake District and rightly so! Not only does it have a strong connection with the famous Poet Laureate William Wordsworth (see Walk 6), but it has an intrinsic charm of its own. It welcomes visitors from all over the world and provides information leaflets in Japanese as well as European languages. The graves of Wordsworth, his wife Mary and members of his family, located to the east of the church, undoubtedly have great drawing power.

The church is situated in the heart of this popular village, by the River Rothay, and slightly overshadowed by the surrounding yew trees, some of which are said to have been planted by Wordsworth himself. An information board by the church gate points out that St Oswald, King of Northumbria, is believed to have preached here before AD642. However, the oldest parts of the present building date from the 14th century.

The first feature within the church that may attract attention is the white wall, divided by a number of arcades that run the length of the nave. This supports a series of timber beams, which in turn sustain the roof. The overall effect is quite curious and Simon Jenkins *(England's Thousand Best Churches)* considers it to be "zany". However, the explanation is that an additional nave was added when the church was extended between 1490 and 1500, and in 1562 a single overarching roof replaced the two roofs. The north aisle is referred to as the "Langdale aisle" as worshippers from that area were first seated there.

There are a considerable number of commemorative wall tablets in the church. Wordsworth's own memorial is behind the choir stalls on the north wall of the main nave. It is relatively simple and low key compared to some of the others, for example that of Jemima Anne Deboral almost opposite on the south wall. The Le Flemings, patrons of the church for over 300 years, are

The 'zany' interior of St Oswald, Grasmere *(with the kind permission of the vicar)*

commemorated by wall tablets and the diamond-shaped hatchments that display the family coat of arms on the chancel walls. Opposite the choir stalls is the boxed pew given by Sir Daniel Fleming in 1633 (for the Fleming family, see also Walk 18, St Andrew, Coniston).

Although there is now a stone floor, it has to be remembered that this only dates from the middle of the 19th century. Prior to that period the earthen floor was covered with rushes, a feature recalled in the annual rushbearing ceremony at the beginning of August.

Before leaving the church it is worth taking time to appreciate the effect of the clear, rather than stained glass, east window.

Among the other features of interest are:

❖ The early 18th-century texts' boards that replaced the texts previously painted on the walls themselves.

❖ The exhibition case in the north "Langdale" aisle containing, among other things, Wordsworth's prayer book.

❖ The alms box for the poor of the parish dated 1648 by the curtain of re-membrance on the right of the chancel.

❖ The long handled collection dishes on the south wall by the porch.

❖ The statue of the Madonna and Child by Ophelia Gordon Bell (1915-1975), wife of the artist William Heaton Cooper, on the north wall of the nave.

Information available in the church:

❶ Hand-held information board.

❶ *Grasmere Church.*

❶ *William Wordsworth and St Oswald's Church, Grasmere,* E. Margaret Taylor

❶ *The Rushbearing in Grasmere.*

Grasmere Methodist Church

This is also centrally located in Grasmere village surrounded by shops and holiday accommodation. The door stands open and there is a welcome in English, German and Japanese. This is a good place to experience peace and calm in very simple surroundings. The church was opened in 1874 by the determination of a few stalwart and committed members whose endeavours established it as on-going part of the local community life although it has never had a large membership. During the Second World War many evacuees came to Grasmere and this led to the creation of a thriving Sunday School. In more recent times the church has served the increasing number of holiday makers in the area. It is open for the benefit of visitors every day from Easter to October. Visitors are encouraged to stay a while in the words of a card on the pews:

> "If after Church, you wait awhile
> Someone may greet you with a smile.
> But, if you quickly rise and flee,
> We'll all seem cold and stiff, maybe".

Our Lady of the Wayside RC Church, Grasmere

As its name suggests, this church is outside of the village and by the side of the A591 Keswick to Ambleside road. The traveller is greeted appropriately by the words: "Rest and be thankful" on the church noticeboard. This is, indeed, another fine place to enjoy a tranquil moment.

The church, which was opened in 1965, blends well with its environment as the dominant building material is Lakeland slate. The interior is simple and attractive with the focal point being the centrally placed altar beneath a canopy suspended from the high ceiling. The overall effect is of light and spaciousness. There is little adornment other than the Stations of the Cross, engraved on slate, around the walls, a sculpture of Our Lady of the Wayside and a well known picture entitled *La Madonna Bella.*

The Walks

Walk 27(a), Grasmere and Alcock Tarn: 6 miles

After visiting St Oswald's Church (A) leave via the main gate and turn right towards the centre of the village. Walk to the right of the Moss Grove Hotel, up College Street (the "no entry" road). Grasmere Methodist Church is soon reached on the left-hand side of the road (B).

After visiting the Methodist Church continue to the end of street to the junction. Cross over the road, turn right and walk along the pavement to the

Our Lady of the Wayside RC Church, Grasmere

bridge over the River Rothay. The pavement, now on the other side of the road, takes you over the bridge. Turn right at the Riversdale and the Rothay Lodge to take the public footpath in the direction of Forest Side. The next church soon comes into view ahead. Cross the main road with care and visit the church of Our Lady of the Wayside **(C)**.

After visiting the RC Church, turn right to continue up the quiet lane to pass a series of pleasant dwellings and to reach a T-junction. Turn right, pass Greenbank and follow the public footpath "Greenhead Gill, Alcock Tarn". Go through the waymarked gate at the top of the lane, turn right for Alcock Tarn, cross the footbridge and follow the footpath on the other side. After climbing quite steeply you may care to rest on the bench dedicated to the author of a book, aptly named, *Come for a walk with me* and appreciate the view of Helm Crag ahead. Continue climbing on the clear path and as it winds upwards ignore paths going off to the left. Look out for views of Grasmere on the right. The path is generally well-trodden and stony as it gradually makes its way to reach and pass through the crags. Eventually the climb becomes gentler. A wall appears ahead. Cross the metal gate via a stile and then you are at the substantial Alcock Tarn **(D)**.

Follow the path round the tarn and, almost immediately after the tarn, bear right at a fork in the grassy path to go through a gap in the wall. There are excellent views over to Windermere with glimpses of Elterwater and Coniston as well as an "aerial" view of Grasmere village. Now follow the path downwards. After going through a metal gate at the end of the National Trust

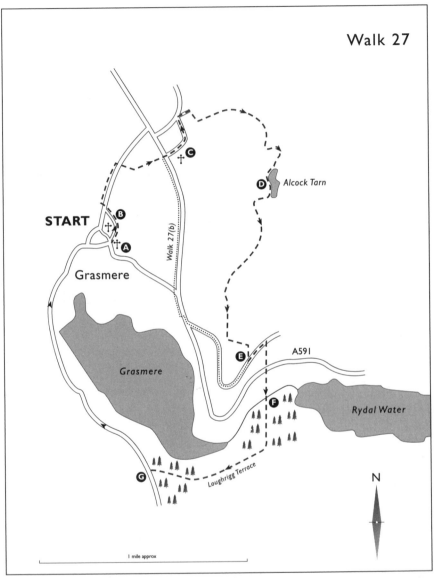

Walk 27

Alcock Tarn

START

Walk 27(b)

Grasmere

Grasmere

A591

Rydal Water

Loughrigg Terrace

N

1 mile approx

Alcock Tarn area, you can enjoy a rest on a well-positioned bench. The descent becomes more gradual as the path winds its way down to enter a plantation. Keep on the main track as it bears left and after passing through two wooden gates the path takes you to a metalled road where you turn left **(E)**.

Continue up the road for 200 metres to some cottages on the left. Turn right to leave the road and follow the stony track down to the main road. Turn left and after a few metres, at the post box, cross the road with care to enter the wood opposite. Follow the path as it bears right past the toilets to cross a short footbridge and soon join a wider path, which leads you to a more substantial footbridge over the River Rothay. Then at a convergence of paths follow the sign straight ahead for the "Woodland Walk to viewpoint on Loughrigg Terrace" **(F)**.

A gentle climb takes you through the wood, which you leave via a kissing gate. Turn right and follow the path to a junction. Bear right and after a few metres Grasmere appears ahead and behind you is Rydal Water. Bear left to follow the public bridleway sign and proceed along Loughrigg Terrace as it contours above the lake. After passing through a metal kissing gate, turn almost immediately right through a wooden kissing gate marked "Grasmere". Follow the broad path as it descends through the wood, passing a cottage, onto a minor road **(G)**.

Turn right and follow the road for just over a mile back to Grasmere Village, St Oswald's Church and the end of the walk.

Walk 27(b), Grasmere only: 4 miles

Follow Walk 27(a) as far as the RC Church **(C)**.

After visiting the church turn left and return to the main road. Turn left and walk for about 1000 metres on the footpath by the side of the A591. Take the lane into Town End to the left of Rose Cottage, just before Dove Cottage (Wordsworth's home from December 1799 until the summer of 1808).

Walk up the lane, passing How Top on your right, and bear left at the junction to walk along the "No through road for motors" under which is a slate slab indicating that this is the way to Rydal. In a short distance the walk rejoins Walk 27(a) at **(E)**. Continue straight ahead and follow the instructions from there to complete the walk.

Walk 28: Low Wray, Colthouse and Hawkshead
Founder, Friends and fleecy burials

Location: St Margaret's Church, (NY372007) is at Low Wray, adjacent to Wray Castle off the B5826 Ambleside to Hawkshead road.

Map: OS Outdoor Leisure 7: The English Lakes South Eastern area.

Distance: Walk 28(a), Low Wray, Colthouse and Hawkshead: 8 miles; Walk 28(b), Low Wray only: 3 miles.

Terrain: Walk 28(a) is mainly along forest paths and over fields with one long ascent. Walk 28(b) follows the initial route along the shore of Windermere and returns on a quiet minor road.

Churches: St Margaret of Antioch, Low Wray; Quaker Meeting House and Burial Ground, Colthouse; St Michael and All Angels, Hawkshead.

Car parking: Parking is available on the roadside near St Margaret's Church, near the entrance to Wray Castle.

The Churches
St Margaret of Antioch, Low Wray

The church lies up a short driveway adjacent to the gatehouse of Wray Castle (see below). With its crenellated tower, you could be forgiven for thinking it was part of the castle itself. The similarity is because both the castle and the church were built at the behest of James Dawson, a retired surgeon; the castle between 1840 and 1847 and the church in 1856. So here is a 19th-century castle with its former chapel, which became a parish church, and which is now a chapel-of-ease of Hawkshead Parish.

The crenellated tower of St Margaret of Antioch, Low Wray

There is a welcome notice on the door and a reminder to visitors to wipe their boots! Inside, this is a neat, narrow church with a high panelled-ceiling. There are some finely carved choir stalls and a complete set of stained glass windows. The atmosphere is decidedly calm and tranquil. The following lines from the church leaflet capture the essence of St Margaret's:

> *"This small church is more than a reminder of past Victorian and Edwardian glories; it is a reminder that, when all else changes, man still needs to step aside from the busy world to pause and think upon the things that are eternal."*

Naturally the Dawsons are commemorated here. James, who died in 1875 at the age of 96, and his wife Margaret who died 13 years earlier are recalled on a tablet on the south wall. Hardwicke Rawnsley, later Canon Rawnsley (see below) was vicar here from 1878 to 1882 and Beatrix Potter was influenced by him when she stayed at Wray Castle as a fifteen-year-old. She subsequently supported his work in the development of the concept of the National Trust.

Among the other features of interest are:

❖ The south-west window which portrays the loss of five children in 1888, presumably the victims of infectious disease.

❖ The brass plaque on the left side of the chancel wall referring to an accident on Lake Windermere.

❖ The north wall has memorials to the fallen in World War I and there is a further memorial plaque on the south wall by the door. The impact of war on the cluster of local families in the neighbourhood, must have been severe as is further evidenced by the fine memorial cross and headstones in the graveyard.

Information available in the church:

❶ A leaflet, *St Margaret of Antioch, Low Wray*, Revd J.P. Inman (revised).

> *Canon Hardwicke Drummond Rawnsley was one of the founders of the National Trust in 1893. He came to the Lake District to become Vicar of Wray in 1877 at the invitation of his cousin Edward Preston Rawnsley who had inherited the estate two years earlier on the death of his uncle Dr James Dawson. Hardwicke Rawnsley campaigned energetically to protect the countryside, for example, from the intrusion of the railway and to keep footpaths open. In 1883 he accepted a move to St Kentigern's at Crosthwaite where he served until 1917 when the death of his first wife Edith and ill health brought about his retirement. He then moved to Grasmere and remarried in 1918. However, he continued with his work for the Church in his capacity as a Canon of Carlisle Cathedral until his death in 1920. He strove tirelessly to defend the environment and to encourage education. He travelled extensively and he was a prolific writer. His story is told in the aptly titled booklet, "The most active volcano in Europe", available in Crosthwaite Church (see Walk 3).*

Quaker Meeting House, Colthouse

Quaker Meeting House and Burial Ground, Colthouse

Strictly speaking this is a meeting house rather than a church as such and it is one of the historic houses of the Society of Friends, dating from 1688. It is beautifully situated within sight of Hawkshead, in farmland known as Benson Orchard. It was bought by the Friends because of its close proximity to the burial ground, which had been in use by them for over thirty years previously. Although the meeting house itself is generally closed, other than for the weekly meeting, you can enter the neat garden and obtain a good view through the windows. It is a very simple white washed building with the date 1688 above the porch entrance.

Inside the porch there is an interesting notice board giving guidance, "To those attending our meeting for the first time". Beneath this there is a brief history of the building and a description of the interior. There are also copies of a leaflet, *Quaker Roots in the North West.*

You can see that the interior has been well-preserved and is largely in its original form. There is a meeting room on one side and a schoolroom on the other side, with a system of moveable panels to convert the two rooms into one, capable of holding 100 people.

The burial ground, which is just a little further down the lane contains very simple headstones of almost uniform design. Many of the inscriptions have faded with age, but those that do remain possess a simplicity that contrasts sharply with the verbose eulogies often encountered elsewhere. The graveyard is obviously well cared for and is still in use, with several plaques on the wall dedicated to more recently deceased members.

St Michael and All Angels, Hawkshead

The church stands in an imposing position just above the heart of the village of Hawkshead, in a very extensive and well-kept churchyard. It is next to the old Grammar School, founded by Edwin Sandys, Archbishop of York in 1585 and attended by the poet Wordsworth from 1779 to 1787.

The present building has developed on the site of a chapel that was apparently built at the beginning of the 13th century by the monks of Furness Abbey. It owes much to the extensions carried out in the 16th century and, in particular, to the endeavours of Archbishop Sandys.

St Michael and All Angels has a solid appearance, both outside and inside, enhanced by the substantial 16th-century oak beams that support the roof of the nave and the high timber ceiling. This structure is underpinned by large white pillars and arcades separating the aisles on both sides of the nave.

A much more recent modification is the re-creation of a chapel in the south-east corner dedicated to St James the Greater, This was established in the late 1960s when space was left by the removal of the organ from that area of the church. Rather fittingly for users of this book, St James is the patron saint of pilgrims and emblems associated with the medieval pilgrims' route to Santiago de Compostela in Spain, such as the cockle shell and staff, together with more modern aids, like rucksacks and boots are embroidered on the kneelers. The feast day of St James, 25 July, was traditionally the rushbearing day when the earthen flooring was covered with fresh rushes.

The church also preserves a collection of "burial in woollen" certificates. These date from the second half of the 16th century when parliament intro-

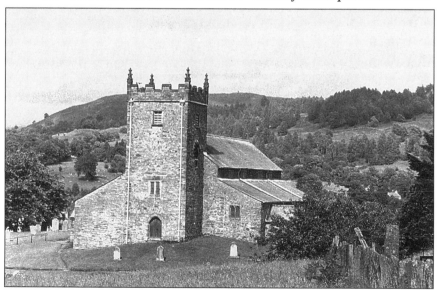

St Michael and All Angels, Hawkshead

duced legislation obliging burials to be in material made from wool in order to protect and encourage the woollen industry, an important part of the economy in this area. (The Visitor Information Centre in Hawkshead contains further interesting information on the subject).

This is a busy church in every sense of the word. The Victorians certainly left their mark through the plethora of plaques and wall tablets that adorn and, to a large extent, have transformed the internal appearance of the original building.

Among the other features of interest are:

❖ The private chapel with a family vault below, built, in the north-east corner, established by Archbishop Sandys in 1585 in memory of his parents.

❖ The framed biblical texts on the walls and the traces of cherub and flower decorations which have been revealed beneath the white washed walls, some of which date from the late 17th century.

❖ The elaborate memorials to the Rawlinsons on the west wall. These were brought from a church in London where Thomas Rawlinson was Lord Mayor. Daniel, his father attended Hawkshead Grammar School.

❖ The old parish records chest in the south-east corner (St James's Chapel).

❖ The exhibits in the showcase which stands on the old funeral trolley by the west wall.

Information available in the church:

❶ Hand-held information board.

❶ *Hawkshead Church, Chapelry and Parish,* T.W. Thompson.

The Walks

Walk 28(a) Low Wray, Colthouse and Hawkshead: 8 miles

After visiting St Margaret's Church **(A)** go back along the driveway and return to the road adjacent to the gatehouse of Wray Castle.

> *Wray Castle now belongs to the National Trust and it is currently rented to a company that provides business training courses, but the grounds are open to the public. An information leaflet describing the history of the castle, together with a suggested walk to view the interesting variety of the trees in the grounds, is available from the reception desk in the foyer of the building.*

Turn left and take the public bridleway immediately on your left by the edge of the wood. Now descend via two gates to the shore of Windermere and the National Trust Claife Estate. Continue along the shoreline for over a mile until you reach Red Nab car park **(B)**.

At the end of the car park keep straight ahead in the direction indicated on the fingerpost "Belle Grange and Ferry". Continue along the lakeshore until you eventually come to a junction where a sign indicates the bridleway to Latterbarrow, Hawkshead and Near Sawrey **(C)**.

Turn right to leave the lake shore on the bridleway, which climbs quite steeply through the forest on a stony path to a waymarked sign "Hawkshead

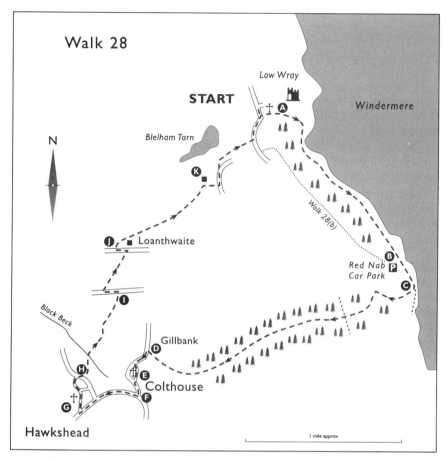

Walk 28

Low Wray

START

Blelham Tarn

Windermere

N

K

Walk 28(b)

J Loanthwaite

I

B
Red Nab **P**
Car Park

C

Black Beck

Gillbank
D

H

E
Colthouse

F

G

Hawkshead

I mile approx

via Guide Posts". Continue ahead on the main track ignoring a track off to the right. At a clearing in the forest, cross the forest track to arrive at a number of signposts/guide posts, and proceed straight ahead in the direction "Hawkshead via Guide Posts" through the high gate. A stony path climbs through the ferns before levelling out, with views of trees on all sides. Go through a further gate to a crossroads of tracks. A sign indicates that the path to Hawkshead is straight ahead and that you are now on the White Post Route at number 10. At number 11, you re-enter the forest through a gate and at long last you can enjoy the gradually descent to Hawkshead. Keep on the clear track as it gradually makes its way downhill, in and out of the trees. Eventually you should get a good view of Hawkshead and St Michael and All Angels' Church on your left. Continue until you meet a minor road at Gillbank **(D)**.

Turn left and after about 200 metres, at the first road junction, follow the sign which takes you off to the left to the Friends Meeting House at

Colthouse. Walk a few hundred metres down the lane to visit the Meeting House **(E)**.

After visiting the Meeting House return to the lane and turn right. Proceed a short distance to pass Town End Farm to meet another quiet road. Turn left and the entrance to the Quaker Burial Ground is a few metres up the slope on your left **(F)**.

After visiting the burial ground return to the road, continue a few metres to a junction and turn right to follow the sign for Hawkshead. Proceed with caution along this slightly busier road, cross the bridge and take the second entrance on your right into Hawkshead to find Wordsworth's old school and the parish church on your left **(G)**.

After visiting the church, turn right as you come out of the porch. Follow the path to the east end of the church and then make your way past the fine war memorial cross (designed by W.G. Collingwood who was also responsible for John Ruskin's memorial at St Andrew, Coniston, see Walk 18). Exit from the churchyard through the metal gate in the north-east corner. Go down the steps and cross the small square diagonally to walk past Brown Cow Cottages and The Queen's Head. Turn right immediately after the Beatrix Potter Gallery down Red Lion Yard to exit onto the main road by a waymarked gate. Cross the busy road with great care and proceed down the lane opposite **(H)**.

Follow the lane as it bears right and then left. Cross the Black Beck via the footbridge, turn left and then bear right to take the path across the meadow to a kissing gate. Continue on the grassy path diagonally right and go through another kissing gate. Turn left at the sign for Loanthwaite and proceed along the clear path over a stile and through a gate onto a lane **(I)**.

Turn left down the lane and proceed for some 70 metres before turning right through a waymarked kissing gate. Now follow the asphalt path with several encouraging waymark signs through two more kissing gates until you meet a lane. Turn left as signposted for Outgate and Low Wray and walk a short way to High Loanthwaite farm **(J)**.

Past the farm buildings, turn immediately right through a gate at the fingerpost to Outgate and High Tock How. Walk along the public footpath, passing a further sign for High Tock How and High Wray, keeping in the same direction through the occasional gates and following the waymarks until you reach a dyke. At the dyke follow the signs, left then right, to cross it near the fence. Now continue on the faint path over two adjacent stiles. Proceed in the same direction, making your way through the reeds and following the waymark posts as you aim for the left-hand corner of the stone wall which appears ahead. Near the wall you should pick up a vehicle track which leads ahead with the wall on your right. Blelham Tarn comes into view to your left and Windermere appears ahead. Continue ahead towards the farm to a stile near a fingerpost "Public footpath High Tock How" **(K)**.

Cross the stile and follow the track to take another stile next to a gate. Follow the National Trust footpath sign directing you to Wray to join a minor road and follow it as it bears left. Walk down the road for about 100 metres and, at the bottom of the hill, leave the road, as it bears right, to carry straight on in front of the cottages. Follow the sign to Wray Castle via an old stone stile next to a gateway and pass through a gate to walk along the track above the tarn. Continue ahead via the waymarked stiles and posts round the side of pasture lands with a wire fence and hedge on your right eventually to skirt some trees, also on your right. The path then takes you through some trees and a kissing gate to cross a footbridge. Again continue ahead in the direction of the waymark posts through a gate and onto a quiet road. Turn left and follow the road up past The Old Vicarage back to the church at Wray and the end of the walk.

Walk 28(b), Low Wray only: 3 miles

Follow Walk 28(a) as far as to Red Nab car park **(B)**. At the exit to the car park, turn right up the metalled road. Climb steadily away from the lake shore through the woods for about a mile. At the T-junction turn right to pass through Wray and follow the road for about 800 metres back to the church and the end of the walk.

Walk 29: Troutbeck and Ambleside
Morris, mountain and mural

Location: Jesus Church (NY413028) is on the outskirts of Troutbeck on the A592 Penrith to Ulverston road, near Ambleside.

Distance: Walk 29(a), Troutbeck and Ambleside: 8 miles; Walk 29(b), Troutbeck only: 2½ miles.

Map: OS Outdoor Leisure 7: The English Lakes South Eastern area.

Terrain: This is practically all on public footpaths and bridleways with very short sections on quiet country lanes. There are several long climbs and descents on Walk 29(a).

Churches: Jesus Church, Troutbeck; St Mary the Virgin, Ambleside.

Car parking: There is parking some 200 metres down from the Jesus Church, off the A592, on the minor road to Troutbeck at Church Bridge.

The Churches
Jesus Church, Troutbeck

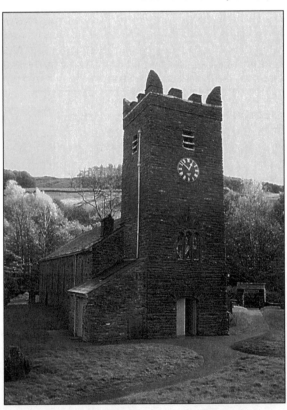

The unusually named Jesus Church, Troutbeck

Instead of being dedicated to a patron saint, this church is very unusually named the Jesus Church. It stands on its own by the side of the A592, a short distance from the Kirkstone Pass and a few hundred metres below the village of Troutbeck. The tower above the west door bears the date 1736 when the church was largely rebuilt on the site of a 16th-century mountain chapel. There have been several restorations and refurbishments since then and so very little of the earlier building remains. However, it is believed that the impressive beams which underpin the roof came from the 16th-century church.

Walkers are obviously regular visitors here and a notice politely requests you not to spoil the light coloured carpet with your muddy boots! However, you are clearly welcome here with a greeting:

"Friend; this church doth open stand for thee
That thou mayest Sit, Rest, Think and Pray"

The major attractions here are probably the 19th-century stained glass windows, especially the east window, the composite work of three distinguished Victorian artists: William Morris, Sir Edward Burne-Jones and Ford Maddox Brown. They are thought to have first visited the area on a fishing trip and then each been responsible for a different section of the window. Details of this and the other windows are available in the church.

The old stone steps that lead from the porch to the gallery are worth climbing (with care). You will find there the coat of arms of George II, painted in 1737, a reminder to parishioners of their loyalty to the English crown. There is also an old notice board from St Andrew's church at Low Troutbeck, a mission church, no longer in regular use, on the Windermere to Ambleside road. From the gallery there is a fine view of the wooden beams and the east window.

In keeping with the Victorian tradition, there are many plaques and dedicated windows in memory of local families and there is evidence that Troutbeck was fond of its vicars. The church is also rightly proud of the impressive number of its parishioners who served in the two world wars and they are remembered both at the top of the stone stairs and in the porch. There is also a fine Lakeland stone memorial cross in the churchyard.

Among the other features of interest are:

❖ The parish chest by the font, used to keep the parish records, with its three locks, one for the vicar and on each for the two churchwardens.

❖ The fine carved communion rails and the oak panelling in the chancel, introduced in 1958 from Calgarth Hall, Windermere and thought to be of early 17th-century origin.

❖ The elaborate stone tablet on the south wall referring to money bequeathed to provide bread for the poor.

❖ The very pleasant churchyard with its three lych-gates. It is well provided with benches and there is a bird box trail for families.

Information available in the church:

❶ There are information boards about the church and the windows at the back of the church.

❶ *Jesus Church Troutbeck.*

❶ *Troutbeck Village Guide*, Margaret Parsons.

St Mary the Virgin, Ambleside

This church, unlike the Jesus Church at Troutbeck, is clearly in an urban location, albeit tucked away in a quiet corner of Ambleside, a few hundred metres from the main tourist area. It is a large church built in the 1850s, shortly after the arrival of the railway to Windermere, by those far sighted enough to anticipate the growth of tourism to the Lake District. However, it was not the first church to serve this area and it eventually replaced nearby St Anne's which in turn had superseded the mountain chapel on Chapel Hill dating from the end of the 16th century.

The tall and imposing spire is eye catching, giving a hint of Victorian finery and opulence that contrasts with the more rugged church buildings generally found in the Cumbrian valleys. However, it appears that the weight of the spire has placed a burden on the tower and on the pockets of the parishioners!

A notice welcomes the visitor in five languages and there is a warm invitation:

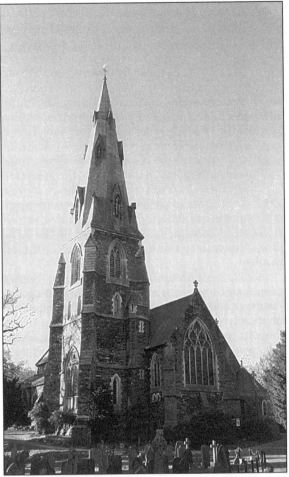

The weighty spire of St Mary the Virgin, Ambleside

"Please come in and enjoy the beauty and peace of this much-loved church".

Statistics indicate that more than 300 people from over 33 countries visited St Mary's in 1999, a figure that perhaps can only be rivalled by the likes of Grasmere, Hawkshead and Cartmel Priory. However, perhaps due to the spaciousness of the interior, there is a calm and peaceful atmosphere as visitors quietly come and go.

Although William Wordsworth died before this church was built, he contributed money towards it and his widow Mary was present at the dedication ceremony in 1854. He is remembered in the Wordsworth Chapel in the north-east corner of the church where the impressive windows were provided by British and American admirers of Wordsworth. Details of the symbolism in these windows and the other windows in the church are provided in the helpful church guide.

There is a large modern mural on the west wall, which depicts the annual rushbearing procession, commemorated as a very popular event in Ambleside. This recalls the time when the earth floors of churches and houses were covered in new rushes several times a year. The mural was painted by Gordon Ransom, a student of the Royal College of Art, which was evacuated here during the World War II. It depicts well-known local characters of the time and there is a helpful explanation beside the mural.

As you may expect from a Victorian church there is an abundance of wall tablets and plaques in memory of benefactors and significant parishioners. The guidebook again is very useful in this respect.

Among the other features of interest are:

❖ The figures of 14 northern saints carved on the front of the choir stalls. The guidebook contains a key to these.

❖ The stone reredos behind the altar in the north east corner (Wordsworth Chapel) and the modern sculpture of the Virgin and Child on a window sill in the south aisle, both by Josephina de Vasconcellos, the highly regarded sculptor who made her home in Ambleside (see also Walk 13, Greystoke Church and Walk 24, Cartmel Priory).

❖ The sandstone font in front of the chancel steps which was found in St Anne's Church and is thought to be pre-Reformation, although the base and stand are more recent.

❖ The fine war memorial which stands on a small mound outside the north porch. The churchyard itself is extensive and well cared for.

Information available in the church:

❶ Hand-held information boards.

❶ *Parish Church of St Mary the Virgin, Ambleside in the Diocese of Carlisle.*

The Walks

Walk 29(a), Troutbeck and Ambleside: 8 miles

After visiting Jesus Church, Troutbeck (**A**), turn right as you leave the porch and follow the path through the gate and out of the churchyard. Turn left and, after about 50 metres, leave the main path to cross a waymarked stile on your right between two gates. Go up the grassy bank and proceed on the clear path through three kissing gates to reach an intersection of paths. Continue straight ahead on a metalled lane in the direction signposted "Public bridleway High Green". Turn left at the T-junction and pass (or better still visit!) the Mortal Man hotel (**B**).

Bear left along the minor road and, after about 150 metres, turn right at Lanefoot Farm House in the direction of the public footpath sign to Nanny Lane (**C**).

Go through the gate and follow the path on the steady steep pull up from

Troutbeck. Eventually, when the track levels off, you cross a stile next to a gate and then, after a few hundred metres, you leave Nanny Lane through a large metal kissing gate on your left by a sign "Footpath to Ambleside via Wansfell" **(D)**.

Now the way is clear and it is only a question of keeping to the path, passing a waymark post, a metal kissing gate and a couple of small cairns and persisting with the long climb which takes you via several false summits to Wansfell just beyond a ladder stile. Here, clouds permitting, you will be rewarded with excellent views of Windermere, Rydal, Grasmere, Elterwater and the Langdales beyond **(E)**.

From the stile, walk straight ahead and bear left round the crag. The path can be slippery and due care is needed. The way to Ambleside is now clear. The path is rocky and stepped and zig-zags down the long descent passing through a gap in a wall. You can always give your knees a rest by stopping to admire the views and to identify Ambleside church with its distinctive spire. Eventually after crossing a small footbridge, you reach a stone wall. Turn right, go through the kissing gate and continue down on the surfaced path, with the Stock Ghyll Beck on your right. Soon you cross a stile and go down some slate steps on to a tarmac road. Turn left and continue down the tree lined road. Shortly after passing St Martin's College, Kelsick, take the road off to the left by the almost concealed public footpath sign. Proceed between the fine beech hedges and soon look out for a metal kissing gate on the right signed "Public footpath to The Gale, Lake Rd". Go through the gate and follow the narrow path via a metal gate and a waymark onto another road. Turn right and descend until the road bears left, where you continue straight ahead down a stepped path, between the houses, to meet the busy streets of Ambleside opposite The Homes of Football (!).Cross over the road with care, continue in the same direction down Kelsick Street opposite and make your way to Ambleside Parish Church, which lies ahead **(F)**.

After visiting the church retrace your steps down the drive and turn right at the crossroads. Continue along the pavement for a few hundred metres until you pass the Ambleside Lodge hotel. Now cross the busy road with care, especially as the traffic is two-way at this point, and continue along the pavement on the other side until you are opposite the road junction to Coniston, Hawkshead and Langdale. Here you go through the kissing gate on your left to take the public footpath, which leads up a narrow lane and via another stile next to a gate soon to meet the main road (A591) opposite the Fisherbeck Hotel. Cross the road with great care and proceed straight ahead between the beck and the car park to meet a minor road **(G)**.

Turn right and continue for about 150 metres behind the cottages to take a steep road off to the left by Lane Foot Cottage signposted "Jenkins Crag-Skelghyll and Troutbeck (Bridleway)". The route back to Troutbeck consists mainly of a long, gradual climb but the views are rewarding. At Strawberry Bank keep on the lower road for Jenkyn Crag and Skelghyll Woods. Keep on the main track and don't be tempted to take a path off to the

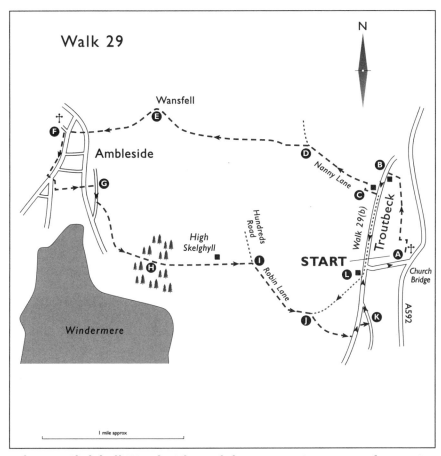

Walk 29

N

Wansfell **E**

F †

Ambleside

G

D

Nanny Lane

B

C

Troutbeck

Walk 29(b)

Hundreds Road

High Skelghyll

O

START

A †

Church Bridge

L

Robin Lane

H

Windermere

J

K

A592

I mile approx

right into Skelghyll Woods. The path becomes quite steep and stony just before you cross a bridge at a sign for Jenkin Crag, Skelgill (both spelt in various ways) and Troutbeck. It is worthwhile diverting slightly to enjoy the splendid views over Windermere at Jenkyn Crag **(H)**.

Continue on the path ahead until, after passing through a number of gates as well as the farmyard at High Skelghyll, you reach a metalled track. Follow the track and at a fork bear left to go through the kissing gate next to a cattle grid. Cross the beck and turn immediately left to pass through a waymarked gate and then another gate. Proceed ahead along the path as it climbs then momentarily descends to ford a beck. Then after two kissing gates another track, the Hundreds Road, joins from the left as you continue ahead between the stone walls now on Robin Lane **(I)**.

After about 400 metres, just before a bend and with a bench on the corner you arrive at a clear fork **(J)**.

Take the right fork to descend a stony track to meet a minor road. Turn left along the road and then, after about 100 metres, leave the road to take a waymarked bridleway on your right down a leafy lane. Go through a gate and pass between two cottages to meet a further minor road at Ford Lane Barn (**K**).

Turn left and ascend into the village, bearing right at the junction opposite the National Trust's Townend property and continue to reach the Post Office (**L**). Continue ahead a short distance, turn right at the junction and walk down the road for a few hundred metres, passing The Old Vicarage, to return to the church and the end of the walk.

Walk 29(b), Troutbeck only: 2½ miles

Follow the route of the Walk 29(a) from Jesus Church, Troutbeck, past the Mortal Man hotel as far as Lanefoot Farm (**C**). At this point you continue straight ahead and enjoy the views of Troutbeck. The W.I. village guidebook (available in Jesus Church) is very helpful in identifying the buildings. Continue as far as the Post Office (**L**). This is part of the village institute building with its fine millennium clock, in memory of a former postmistress. Bear right to leave the road along a waymarked bridlepath to Robin Lane. Shortly after passing some cottages you find yourself between the stone walls of Robin Lane. After about 1000 metres or so, as you pass a bench on your left, take the stony track that descends to the left (**J**). Now follow the way back to Troutbeck and its church as described for Walk 29(b).

Walk 30: Witherslack
Prelate, perpendicular! and plantations

Location: St Paul's Church (SD 432842) is on the outskirts of Witherslack village. Witherslack is on a minor road, to the north of the A590, 6 miles east of Newby Bridge.

Distance: 8½ miles.

Map: OS Outdoor Leisure 7: The English Lakes South Eastern area.

Terrain: Mainly on public footpaths through forests and open countryside. Most of the walk is gently undulating but there is a very steep ascent in the early stages.

Church: St Paul, Witherslack.

Car parking: There is car parking outside the church.

The Church

The church of St Paul is pleasantly situated near to woods and with views over the Winster Valley. It was built around 1649, in the period following the restoration of Charles II, with a bequest from John Barwick, Dean of St Paul's Cathedral. John and his brother Peter who was physician to Charles II were born in Witherslack. The local school, a few hundred metres to the south of the church, is called Dean Barwick Primary School.

The church has a west tower and a long single chamber nave and chancel. It is a good example of the Gothic style of the Restoration period – a workmanlike building set between ancient yew trees in its well-kept graveyard. Extensive renovation carried out in 1768 included heightening the nave and chancel together with a match-

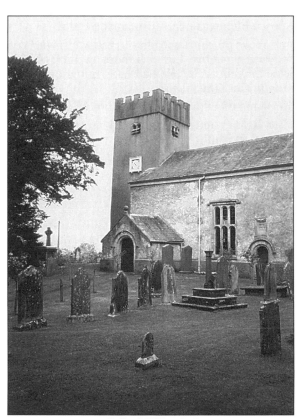

St Paul, Witherslack

ing extension of the plain glass side windows by adding transoms and upper halves. The tower clock was converted to electric power in 1961 but retains the 1768 face with its single pointer.

Interior renovation in 1768 included the addition of two columns to give a better defined sanctuary. The wide nave combined with the raised ceiling and long plain glass windows creates a sense of spaciousness. However, not all commentators are taken with the overall effect, Frank Welsh (*The Companion Guide to The Lake District*) considers that the 18th-century remodelling "resembles nothing more than the ballroom of a country house of the period".

There are wall tablets and other memorials, mostly to the Stanley family, Earls of Derby and lords of the manor of Witherslack since 1485.

Among the other features of interest are:

❖ In the baptistry, the oak panelling given by Sandford School, which used to be in Witherslack Hall, on the occasion of the school's centenary.

❖ The font from 1666, of which the lower half might be earlier, and the cover from the Chapel of St Mary which was near Witherslack Hall.

❖ The Barwick coat of arms, above the entrance door in the south west corner, incorporating the red rose given by Charles II in recognition of Dean Barwick's help in restoring the monarchy. He had been imprisoned for a number of years for acting in the King's cause.

❖ The war memorial in the shape of a cross on the south wall.

❖ The east window with five lights including stained glass armorial bearings of the Barwick and Stanley families.

Information available in the church:

❶ Hand-held information board.

The Walk

Leave the church **(A)** and grounds by the gate on the south side leading to the car parking area. Walk across the area and cross the road to the public footpath sign opposite the hotel. Go into the woods and climb up the path, which turns left and bends back to meet a broad path at a junction marked by a mini-cairn. Turn left and walk uphill and carry on, ignoring a waymarked path off to the right. At a crossing of paths, continue in the same direction as indicated by the blue waymark. The path levels off before coming to a waymarked gate. Go through the gate and turn right to follow the direction shown by the waymark, and on to an open area with some craggy outcrops. Follow the path as it passes the waymark posts. The path becomes quite boggy as it skirts the edge of a wood and comes to a waymarked gate. There are two houses ahead. Go through the gate and bear left in the direction of the bridleway sign passing Lawns House on your right. A waymark post directs you through a gate and onto a farm track. Follow this track for a few hundred metres to Witherslack Hall Farm **(B)**.

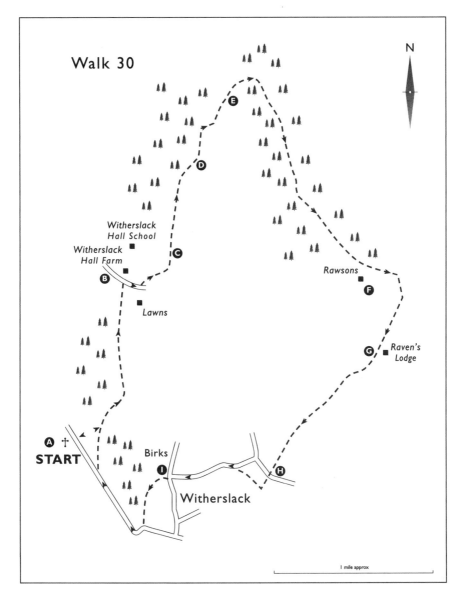

Walk 30

Witherslack
Hall School

Witherslack
Hall Farm

Lawns

Rawsons

Raven's
Lodge

Birks

START

Witherslack

1 mile approx

Turn right onto the narrow metalled road and walk downhill. You come to
the entrance to Witherslack Hall School and need, immediately, to look out
for the public footpath sign "Whitbarrow". Turn left onto this footpath. As
you walk along you can catch a glimpse of the school building over to your
left, before arriving at a waymarked gate and a notice board with information
about Whitbarrow Scar Nature Reserve, which is ahead. Go left onto the

sports field via a stile and follow the waymark sign across the end of the field and then go through the gap in the wall and follow the waymark direction into the woods (C).

From this point there is a steady climb, which is very steep in places, up a waymarked path through the trees. You arrive at a waymarked stile via a gap in a wall. Go over the stile to come to a notice board which states "National Nature Reserve. The Wild Life Trust Cumbria". Behind are magnificent views of the wooded valley bottom with Witherslack Hall School in its clearing. Carry on the path for the short distance to reach a broad, undulating plateau (D).

Again looking back the view is spectacular taking in the Winster Valley with Cartmel Fell on the right. The summit of Whitbarrow lies across the plateau in a forest. Follow the path for several hundred metres to arrive at a series of cairns and carry on as it wends its way, climbing a little, past the cairns to arrive at the most imposing cairn dedicated to the memory of Canon G.A.K. Hervey (1893 – 1967) founder of the Lake District Naturalists' Trust (E).

Past the cairn, continue on the path which bears left and passes flat rock formations on your right. Keep to the path that heads for the woods ahead and then turns alongside the woods with the trees and a wall on your right. When you come to another information board go over the stone stile on your right into the woods. Walk straight ahead. After 200 metres a narrow path goes off to the left – ignore this and carry on to descend a short way to come to a junction of paths. Turn left and continue on the forest track for about 800 metres and at another junction turn right. The path runs mostly downhill to another junction where you need to turn right as indicated by the waymark post. Continue along this more or less level path passing two waymark posts and after about 800 metres come to a junction with a forest track. Turn right as indicated by the waymark and walk along the wide track. Just after a gateway in a stone wall, look out for the waymark on the right. Turn left as indicated and follow the path as it runs along the edge of the woodland. Over to your left the broad Lyth Valley comes into view and Levens village can be seen in the distance. Keep to the path as it descends, zig-zags right and left, then crosses a ladder stile. Follow the track to reach the farm buildings of Rawsons on your right (F).

Walk past the farm and turn right to follow the farm road. In a short while there are trees on your right. Continue along the road with the cliffs of White Scar towering above you on the right, to reach Raven's Lodge (G).

Some 20 metres or so after the road bears left around Raven's Lodge farm, cross the road to a public bridleway sign. Go through two waymarked gates into the trees and keep to the path as it ascends quite steeply. The path is stony for several hundred metres or so before joining a metalled road at the imposing gateway of Whitbarrow Lodge. Walk in the same direction along the road for 100 metres and turn left onto the public footpath. Follow the narrow path that descends between trees and through a waymarked gate and becomes a broad grassy track as it approaches farm buildings. Go through the gate into the farm area, turn left and exit via a gate onto a farm road. Proceed along this road to a junction with a minor road (**H**).

Cross the road and take the public footpath to "Bull Bridge" through the farm yard and exit into a field. Walk across the field passing a waymarked telegraph pole to come to a waymarked gate. Proceed in the direction indicated to pass a house on your right and go through a kissing gate. Go over the gravel driveway and bear right, behind the greenhouse. Continue on a narrow path for a short distance between trees and exit into a field via a waymarked gate. Bear left in the direction of the waymark towards the woods ahead passing a rocky outcrop on your right. Cross the stream by the little stone footbridge then through a kissing gate to bear right through the wood. Continue, past North View Cottage, and after a short distance emerge onto a metalled road at Ghyll Cottage and a small hamlet. Turn left, cross the bridge over the stream and then turn right at the junction at Bull Farm House. Keep on the minor road for 800 metres or so until you arrive at a junction, with Birks Farm on the other side of the road (**I**).

Turn left and then almost immediately cross the road to the public footpath sign. Go through the gates of Birks Farm and proceed along the farm track to pass the farm house on your right. Go between the farm house buildings to a waymarked metal gate near a beck. Go through the gate and bear left along a clear track to cross a waymarked stile near a gate. Continue up the track with a wood on the right and then proceed up the side of a field. Go through a waymarked kissing gate near a shed at the corner of the field. After a few metres bear left in the direction of a waymarked post and go up the grassy path to pass a house on your left to exit onto a road. Turn right and walk up the road for about 120 metres to pass The Croft on your right and after another 20 metres take the public bridleway "Witherslack Hall" on your right. Climb gradually on the clear path through the woods for about 800 metres. Look out for the mini-cairn on your left, which was encountered at the beginning of the walk. Turn left to retrace your steps down to the church and the end of the walk.

Bibliography

Betjeman J. (1993), *Sir John Betjeman's Guide to English Parish Churches*, 2nd ed., Harper Collins.

Bouch, C.M.L. (1981), *Prelates and People of the Lake Counties: A History of the Diocese of Carlisle 1133-1953*,Titus Wilson & Son Ltd., Kendal.

Davies, Hunter (1995), *Wainwright: The Biography*, Michael Joseph.

Davies, Hunter (1997), *William Wordsworth: A Biography*, revised ed., Sutton Publishing.

Jenkins, Simon (1999), *England's Thousand Best Churches*, Allen Lane: The Penguin Press.

Kempe, Hilary (1975), *The Jacobite Rebellion*, Almark Publishing.

Marsh, Terry (1999), *Towns and Villages of Britain: Cumbria*, Sigma Leisure.

Mitchell, W.R., (1999), *Sacred Places of the Lake District: A Handbook for Holiday Pilgrims*, Castleberg.

Moorman, J.R.H. (1980), *A History of the Church in England*, A & C Black.

Owen, Hugh (1990), *The Lowther Family*, Phillimore.

Pevsner, Nikolaus (1967), *The Buildings of England: Cumberland and Westmorland*, Penguin Books.

Pevsner, Nikolaus (1969), *The Buildings of England: North Lancashire*, Penguin Books.

Price, H.A.L. (1967), *Lake District Portraits*, Harvill Press.

Ramshaw, David (1996), *The English Lakes: Tales from History, Legend and Folklore*, P3 Publications.

Salter, Mike (1998), *The Old Parish Churches of Cumbria*, Folly Publications.

Size, Nicholas (1930), *The Secret Valley*, Frederick Warne.

Thomas, M.F. (1999), *A History of Tottlebank Baptist Church*, Tottlebank Baptist Church.

Welsh, Frank (1997), *The Companion Guide to The Lake District*, 2nd ed., Collins.